The Development of Industrial Society Series

Edward Bulwer-Lytton

# ENGLAND AND THE ENGLISH

Volume 2

IRISH UNIVERSITY PRESS

Shannon   Ireland

First edition London 1833
Second edition London 1833
Third edition London and New York 1876


This I U P reprint is a photolithographic facsimile of
the second edition and is unabridged, retaining the
original printer's imprint.


© *1971 Irish University Press Shannon Ireland*


*All forms of micropublishing*
© *Irish University Microforms Shannon Ireland*


ISBN 0 7165 1592 X Two volumes

ISBN 0 7165 1593 8 Volume 1

ISBN 0 7165 1594 6 Volume 2

*T M MacGlinchey Publisher*

*Irish University Press Shannon Ireland*


PRINTED IN THE REPUBLIC OF IRELAND BY
ROBERT HOGG PRINTER TO IRISH UNIVERSITY PRESS

# ENGLAND

### AND

# THE ENGLISH.

---

## VOL. II.

LONDON: PRINTED BY S. BENTLEY, DORSET STREET.

# ENGLAND

### AND

# THE ENGLISH.

## BY EDWARD LYTTON BULWER, ESQ. M.P.

### AUTHOR OF "PELHAM," "DEVEREUX," AND "EUGENE ARAM."

---

" Ordine gentis
" Mores, et studia, et populos, et prælia dicam."     VIRGIL.

" Every now and then we should examine ourselves; self-amendment is the offspring of self-knowledge. But foreigners do not *examine* our condition; they only glance at its surface. Why should we print volumes upon other countries and be silent upon our own? Why traverse the world and neglect the phenomena around us? Why should the spirit of our researches be a lynx in Africa and a mole in England? Why, in one word, should a nation be never criticised by a native?"     MONTAGU.

---

### SECOND EDITION.

### IN TWO VOLUMES.
### VOL. II.

## LONDON:

### RICHARD BENTLEY, NEW BURLINGTON STREET.

### 1833.

# CONTENTS.

## BOOK THE FOURTH.

### VIEW OF THE INTELLECTUAL SPIRIT OF THE TIME.

INSCRIBED TO J. D'ISRAELI, ESQ.

## CHAPTER III.

## CHAPTER IV.

### STYLE.

## CHAPTER VIII.

### THE STATE OF SCIENCE.

## CHAPTER IX.

### THE STATE OF THE ARTS.

## CHAPTER X.

### SUPPLEMENTARY CHARACTERS.

## BOOK THE FIFTH.

### A VIEW OF OUR POLITICAL STATE.

#### INSCRIBED TO THE ENGLISH PEOPLE.

### CHAPTER I.

### CHAPTER II.

## CHAPTER VII.

## CHAPTER VIII.

## CHAPTER THE LAST.

## APPENDIX.

# BOOK THE FOURTH.

# VIEW OF THE INTELLECTUAL SPIRIT OF THE TIME.

INSCRIBED TO

## J. D'ISRAELI, ESQ.

AUTHOR OF "THE CURIOSITIES OF LITERATURE," AND "THE LITERARY CHARACTER," ETC.

——" Inter sylvas Academi quærere verum."

HOR. EP.

VOL. II.

# VIEW OF THE INTELLECTUAL SPIRIT OF THE TIME.

## INSCRIBED TO J. D'ISRAELI, ESQ.

---

## CHAPTER I.

The Influence of the Press—Is the Influence rather of Opinion than of Knowledge—Its Voice more true with respect to Things than Persons —The Duke of Wellington's Horse *versus* Lord Palmerston's—The Press represents—Whom ?—Those who buy it !—Important Deduction from this Fact—Not the Poor, but the Hangers on of the Rich who buy the Scurrilous papers—The Valet and the Mechanic—If one Part of the Press *represents*, another Part *originates* Opinion—The preservation of the anonymous in Periodicals—Its effects—Difference between a French Editor and an English—Why is the Press Anti-aristocratic ?—Effects of Removing the Newspaper Duties—The Intellectual Spirit of the Times—Eastern Tradition.

PERMIT me, my dear sir, to honour with your name that section of my various undertaking, which involves an inquiry into the Intellectual Spirit of the Time. I believe that you employ the hours of a serene and dignified leisure in the composition of a work that, when completed, will fill no inconsiderable vacuum in English Literature; namely, the History of English Literature itself. Of the arrival of that work, you wish us to consider those classical and most charming essays which you have already given to the world, merely as precursors—specimens of a great whole—which ought, in justice to your present reputation, to add a permanent glory to the letters of your country. It will therefore, perhaps, afford to you a pleasurable interest, to survey the literary aspect of these times, into which your chronicle must merge, and to wander, even with an erring guide, beside those Rivers of Light, which you have tracked to their distant source, with all the perseverance of the antiquarian, and all the enthusiasm of the scholar.

Before, however, I can invite you to the more attractive part of my subject ;—before we can rove at will among the gardens of Poesy, or the not less delightful mazes of that Philosophy, which to see is to adore ; before the domains of Science and of Art can receive our exploring footsteps, we must pause awhile to examine the condition of that mighty, though ambiguous, Power by which the time receives its more vivid impressions, and conveys its more noisy opinions. As a preliminary to our criti-

cisms on the productions of the Press, we will
survey the nature of its influence ;—and pro-
pitiate with due reverence the sibyl who too
often commits

> Her prophetic mind
> To fluttering leaves, the sport of every wind,

ere we can gain admittance to the happy souls,

> In groves who live, and lie on mossy beds,
> By crystal streams that murmur through the meads ;

> —————————Choro pæana canentes
> Inter odoratum lauri nemus.

Hitherto I have traced, in the various branches
of my inquiry, the latent and pervading influence of an aristocracy ;—I am now about to examine the nature of that antagonist power which
is the only formidable check that our moral relations have yet opposed to it. Much has been
said in a desultory manner respecting the influence of the Press ; but I am not aware of
any essay on the subject which seems written
with a view rather to examine than declaim.
" Vous l'allez comprendre, j'espère, si vous
m'écoutez,—il est fête, et nous avons le temps
de causer."—I shall go at once to the heart of
the question, and with your permission, we will
not throw away our time by talking much on
the minor considerations.

It is the habit of some persons more ardent

than profound, to lavish indiscriminate praises on the press, and to term its influence, the influence of Knowledge—it is rather the influence of Opinion. Large classes of men entertain certain views on matters of policy, trade, or morals. A newspaper supports itself by addressing those classes; it brings to light all the knowledge requisite to enforce or illustrate the views of its supporters; it embodies also the prejudice, the passion, and the sectarian bigotry that belong to one body of men engaged in active opposition to another. It is therefore the organ of opinion; expressing at once the truths and the errors, the good and the bad, of the prevalent opinion it represents.

Thus it is impossible to expect the newspaper you consider right in regard to sentiments to be fair in regard to persons. Supposing it expresses the *facts* which belong to knowledge, they are never stated with the *impartiality* that belongs to knowledge.—" Heavens! my dear sir! have you heard the report? The Duke of Wellington's horse has run over a poor boy!" A whig paper seizes on the lamentable story—magnifies, enlarges on it—the Duke of Wellington is admonished—indifference to human life is insinuated. The tory paper replies: it grants the fact, but interprets it differently: the fool of a boy was decidedly in the way—the brute of a horse had a mouth notoriously as hard as a brickbat—the rider himself was not to blame —what unheard-of malignity, to impute as a reproach to the Duke of Wellington, a misfortune only to be attributed to the eyes of the boy, and the jaw-bone of the horse! But bless me! a new report has arisen :—it was not the Duke of Wellington's horse that ran over the boy; it was Lord Palmerston's. It is now the tory journal's opportunity to triumph. What perversion in the lying whig paper !—and what atrocity in Lord Palmerston! All the insinuations that were so shameful against the duke are now profusely directed against the viscount. The very same interpretations that the tory paper so magisterially condemned, are now by the tory paper unreservedly applied. The offence of distortion is equally continued—it is only transferred from one person to another. This is a type of the power of the press: its very enforcement of opinions prevents its being just as to persons. Facts, indeed, are stated, but the interpretation of facts is always a matter of dispute. And thus to the last chapter, it is easier to obtain a just criticism of the merits of the drama, than of the qualities of the actors. Long after the public mind has decided unani-

mously with respect to measures, it remains
doubtful and divided with regard to the characters of men.   In this the press is still the
faithful record of Opinion, and the ephemeral
Journal is the type of the everlasting History !

Newspapers being thus the organ of several
opinions, the result is, the influence of opinion ;
because, that newspaper sells the best which
addresses itself to the largest class ; it becomes
influential in proportion to its sale, and thence,
the most popular opinion grows, at last, into
the greatest power.

But from this arises a profound consideration,
not hitherto sufficiently enforced.   The newspaper represents opinion ; but the opinion of
whom ?—*those persons among whom it chiefly
circulates.*   What follows ?—why, that the price
of the newspaper must have a considerable influence on the expression of opinion : because,
according to the price would be the extent of
its circulation ; and, according to the opinion of
the majority of its supporters, would be the
current opinion of the paper.

Supposing it were possible to raise the price
of all the daily newspapers to two shillings each,
what would be the consequence ?—that a vast
number of the poorer subscribers would desert
whatever journal they had been accustomed

to read, that the circle of its supporters
would become limited to those who could afford
its price. It would then be to the opinions and
interests of this small and wealthy class, that it
could alone address itself; if it did not meet
their approbation, it could not exist; their
opinion would be alone represented, the opinion of the mass would be disregarded; and a
newspaper, instead of being the organ of the
*public*, would be the expression of the *oligarchical*, sentiment. Although the aggregate of
property in England is, perhaps, equally divided among the whigs and tories, the *greater
number* of reading persons, possessing property
is alleged to be tory. Supposing the calculation to be correct, the influence of the press
would, by our supposed increase of price, be
at once transferred to the tories; and *The Standard* and *The Albion* would be the most widely
circulated of the daily journals.

If this principle be true, with respect to an
increased price, the converse must be true if the
price were lowered. If the sevenpenny paper
were therefore to sell for twopence, what again
would be the result? Why, the sale being extended from those who can afford sevenpence to
those who can afford twopence, a new majority
must be consulted, the sentiments and desires of

poorer men than at present must be addressed ;
and thus, a new influence of opinion would be
brought to bear on our social relations and our
legislative enactments.

As the extension of the electoral franchise
gave power to the middle classes, so the extended circulation of the press will give power
to the operative. To those who uphold the
principle, that government is instituted for the
good of the greatest number, it is, of course, a
matter of triumph, that the interests of the
greatest number should thus force themselves
into a more immediate voice.*

* In removing the stamp duties, which check one part
of the influence of the press, it would however be conserva-
tive policy to let new sources of enlightenment commence
with the new sources of power. At present, what are called
the taxes on knowledge are in reality, as we have seen before, taxes on opinion. To make opinion knowledge, its
foundation must be laid in instruction. The act which
opens the press should be immediately followed by an act
to organize National Education; and while the people are
yet warm with gratitude for the new boon, and full of confidence to those who give it, care should be taken to secure
for the first teachers of political morals, honest and enlightened men ;—men too, who, having the competent
knowledge, will have the art to express it popularly; not
mere grinders of saws and aphorisms, the pedants of a
system. By this precaution, the appealers to passion will
be met by appealers to interest; and the people will be
instructed as well as warmed. Meanwhile, the system of

It is manifest, that when the eyes of the people are taught steadily to regard their own interests, the class of writing most pleasing to them, will not be that of demagogues; it is probable indeed, that the cheapest papers will seem to the indolent reader of the higher ranks, the most dry and abstruse. For a knowledge of the principles of trade, and of the truths of political economy, is of so vital an importance to the Poor, that those principles and truths will be the main staple of the journals chiefly dedicated to their use. Not engaged in the career of mere amusement that belongs to the wealthy—frivolity, scandal, and the unsatisfying pleasure derived from mere declamation, are not attractive to them. All the great principles of state morals and state policy are derived from one foundation, the *true direction of labour*;—what theme so interesting and so inexhaustible to those "who by labour live?" We may perceive already, by *The Penny Magazine*, what will be the probable character of cheap newspapers addressed to the working classes. The operative finds *The Penny Maga-*

education once begun, proceeds with wonderful rapidity; and, ere the Operative has lost his confidence in the wise government that has granted him the boon of sifting the thoughts of others, his children will have learned the art of thinking for themselves.

*zine* amusing; to the rich man it is the most wearisome of periodicals.

So much for the proud cry of the aristocrat, that the papers to please the rabble must descend to pander the vulgar passions. No! this is the vice of the aristocratic journals, that are supported alone by the excrescences of aristocracy, by gambling-houses, demireps, and valets. The industrious poor are not the purchasers of the *Age.*

A nobleman's valet entertained on a visit his brother, who was a mechanic from Sheffield. The nobleman, walking one Sunday by a newspaper office in the Strand, perceived the two brothers gazing on the inviting announcements on the shopboard, that proclaimed the contents of the several journals; the crowd on the spot delayed him for a moment, and he overheard the following dialogue:

" Why, Tom," said the valet, " see what lots of news there is in this paper !—' Crim. con. extraordinary between a lord and a parson's wife—Jack ———s (Jack is one of our men of fashion, you know, Tom) Adventure with the widow—Scene at Crocky's.' Oh, what fun ! Tom have you got sevenpence ? I 've nothing but gold about *me ;* let's buy this here."

" Lots of news !" said Tom, surlily, " D'ye

call that news? What do I care for your lords and your men of fashion? Crocky! What the devil is Crocky to me? There's much more for my money in this here big sheet: ' Advice to the Operatives—Full report of the debate on the Property Tax—Letter from an emigrant in New South Wales.' That's what *I* calls news."

" Stuff!" cried the valet, astonished.

My lord walked on, somewhat edified by what he had heard.

The scandal of the saloon is news in the pantry; but it is the acts of the legislature that constitute news at the loom.

But, while the main characteristic of the influence of the press is to *represent* opinion, it is not to be denied that it possesses also the nobler prerogative of *originating* it. When we consider all the great names which shed honour upon periodical literature; when we consider, that scarcely a single one of our eminent writers has not been actively engaged in one or other of our journals:—when we remember that Scott, Southey, Brougham, Mackintosh, Bentham, Mill, Macculloch, Campbell, Moore, Fonblanque (and I may add Mr. Southern, a principal writer in the excellent *Spectator,* whose writings obtain a reputation, which, thanks to the custom of the anonymous, is diverted from the writer himself,) have, year after year, been pouring forth in periodical publications, the rich hoard of their thoughts and knowledge ; it is impossible not to perceive that the press, which they thus adorned, only represented in one part of its power the opinions originated in another.

But it is in very rare instances that a daily paper has done more than represent political opinion ; it is the Reviews, quarterly or monthly (and, in two instances, weekly journals) which have aspired to *create* it. And this for an obvious reason : the daily paper looks only to sale for its influence ; the capital risked is so enormous, the fame acquired by contributions to it so small and evanescent, that it is mostly regarded as a mere mercantile speculation. Now *new* opinions are not popular ones ; to swim with the tide, is the necessary motto of opinions that desire to sell : while the majority can see in your journal the daily mirror of themselves, their prejudices and their passions, as well as their sober sense and their true interests, they will run to look upon the reflection. Hence it follows, that the journal which most *represents*, least *originates* opinion, that the two tasks are performed by two separate agents, and that the more new

doctrines a journal promulgates, the less pro-
miscuously it circulates among the public.

In this the moral light resembles the physical, and while we gaze with pleasure on the
objects which reflect the light, the eye shrinks
in pain from the orb which creates it.

A type of that truth in the history of letters,
which declares that the popularity of a writer
consists not in proportion to his superiority over
the public, but in proportion to their sympathy
with his sentiments, may be found in the story
of Dante and the Buffoon; both were entertained at the court of the pedantic Scaliger, the
fool sumptuously, the poet sparely.—" When
will you be as well off as I am?" asked the
fool triumphantly.—" Whenever," was Dante's
caustic reply, " I shall find a patron who resembles *me* as much as Prince Scaliger resembles you."

An originator of opinion precedes the time;
you cannot both precede and reflect it.   Thus,
the most popular journals are Plagiarists of the
Past; they live on the ideas which their more
far-sighted contemporaries propagated ten years
before.   What then was Philosophy, is now
Opinion.

A great characteristic of English periodicals
is the generally strict preservation of secrecy as

to the names of the writers.  The principal advantages alleged in favour of this regard to the
anonymous are three: First, that you can speak
of public men with less reserve ; secondly, that
you can review books with more attention to
their real merits, and without any mixture of
the personal feelings that, if you were known to
the author, might bias the judgment of impartial criticism ; thirdly, that many opinions
you yourself consider it desirable that the public should know, peculiar circumstances of situations, or private checks of timidity and caution,
might induce you to withhold, if your name
were necessarily attached to their publication.
I suspect that these advantages are greatly exaggerated on the one hand, and that their
counterbalancing evils, have been greatly overlooked on the other.

In regard to the first of these advantages, it
is clear that if you can speak of public men
with less reserve, you may speak of them also
with less regard to truth.  In a despotic country, where chains are the reward of free sentiments, the use of the anonymous may be a necessary precaution; but what in this country
should make a public writer shrink from the
open discharge of his duty ?  If his writings be
within the pale of the laws, he has nothing to

fear from an avowal of his name; if without the law, the use of the anonymous does not skreen him. But were your name acknowledged, you could not speak of public men with the same vehement acerbity; you could not repeat charges and propagate reports with the same headlong indifference to accuracy or error. There is more shame in being an open slanderer than a concealed one: you would not, therefore, were your name on the newspaper, insert fragments of " *news*" about persons without ascertaining their foundation in truth: you would not, day after day, like to circulate the stories, which, day after day, you would have the ludicrous task of contradicting.

All this I grant; but, between you and me, dear sir, where is the harm of it? It is well to speak boldly of public men; but to speak what boldly?—not falsehood, but the truth. If the political writer ordinarily affixed his name to his lucubration, he would be brought under the wholesome influence of the same public opinion that he affects to influence or to reflect; he would be more consistent in his opinions,* and

* Many of the political writers, skreened by the anonymous, shift and turn from all opinions, with every popular breath. The *paper* may be abused for it, but the paper is insensate; no one abuses the *unseen writer* of the paper. Thus, there is no shame, because there is no exposure; where there is no shame, there is no honesty.

more cautious in examination. Papers would cease to be proverbial for giving easy access to the current slander and the diurnal lie; and the boldness of their tone would not be the less, because it would be also honest. I have said, to make power safe and constitutional, it must be made responsible; but anonymous power is irresponsible power.

And now, with regard to the second advantage alleged to belong to the use of the anonymous—the advantage in literary criticism: You say that being anonymous, you can review the work more impartially than if the author, perhaps your friend, were to know you to be his critic. Of all arguments in favour of the anonymous, this is the most popular and the most fallacious. Ask any man once let behind the curtain of periodical criticism, and you will find that the very partiality and *respect* to *persons*, which the custom of the anonymous was to prevent, the anonymous especially shields and ensures. Nearly all criticism at this day is the public effect of private acquaintance. When a work has been generally praised in the reviews, even if deservedly, nine times out of ten the author has secured a large connexion with the press. Good heavens! what machinery do we not see exerted to get a book tenderly nursed into vigour. I do not say that the critic is dishonest in this partiality ; perhaps he may be actuated by feelings that, judged by the test of private sentiments, would be considered fair and praiseworthy.

" Ah, poor So-and-so's book ; well, it is no great things ; but So-and-so is a good fellow, I must give him a helping hand."

" C—— has sent me his book to review ; that's a bore, as it's devilish bad ; but as he knows I shall be his critic—I must be civil."

" What, D.'s poems ? it would be d—d unhandsome to abuse them, after all his kindness to me—after dining at his house yesterday."

Such, and a variety of similar, private feelings, which it may be easy to censure, and which the critic himself will laughingly allow you to blame, colour the tone of the great mass of reviews. This veil, so complete to the world, is no veil to the bookwriting friends of the person who uses it. *They* know the hand which deals the blow, or lends the help; and the critic willingly does a kind thing by his friend, because it is never known that in so doing he has done an unjust one by the public. The anonymous, to effect the object which it pretends, must be thoroughly sustained. But in how few cases is this possible ! We have but one Junius

in the world. At the present day there is not a
journal existing in which, while the contributors
are concealed indeed from the world at large,
they are not known to a tolerably wide circle of
publishing friends. Thus, then, in a critical
point of view, the advantages supposed to spring
from the anonymous vanish into smoke. The
mask is worn, not to protect from the petitions of
private partialities, but *to deceive the public as
to the extent to which partiality is carried;* and
the very evils which secrecy was to prevent, it
not only produces, but conceals, and *by* concealment defrauds of a remedy. It is clear, on
more than a superficial consideration, that the
bias of private feelings would be far less strong
upon the tenour of criticism, if the name of the
critic were known ; in the first place, because
the check of public opinion would operate as
a preventive to any reviewer of acknowledged
reputation from tampering with his own honesty ; in the second place, because there are
many persons in the literary world, who would
at once detect and make known to the public
the chain of undue motive that binds the praise
or censure of the critic to the book. Thus you
would indeed, by the publication of the reviewer's name, obtain either that freedom from
private bias, or that counterbalance to its ex-

ercise, of which, by withholding the name, the public have been so grossly defrauded. Were a sudden revelation of the mysteries of the craft now to be made, what—oh what would be the rage, the astonishment, of the public !*

* The influence of certain booksellers upon certain Reviews, is a cry that has been much raised by Reviews in which *those* booksellers had no share. The accusation is as old as Voltaire's time. He complains that booksellers in France and Holland guided the tone of the periodical Reviews : with us, at present, however, the abuse is one so easily detected that I suspect it has been somewhat exaggerated. I know one instance of an influential weekly journal, which was accused, by certain of its rivals, of favouring a bookseller who had a share in its property; yet, accident bringing me in contact with that bookseller, I discovered that it was a matter of the most rankling complaint in his mind, that the editor of the journal, (who had an equal share himself in the journal, and could not be removed,) was so anxious not to deserve the reproach as to be unduly harsh to the books he was accused of unduly favouring: and on looking over the Review, with my curiosity excited to see which party was right, I certainly calculated that a greater proportion of books belonging to the bookseller in question had been severely treated than was consistent with the ratio of praise and censure accorded to the works appertaining to any other publisher. In fact, the moment a journal becomes influential, its annual profits are so considerable, that it would be rarely worth while in any bookseller who may possess a share in it to endanger its sale by a suspicion of dishonesty. The circumstance of his having that share in it is so well known, and the suspicion to which it exposes him so obvious, that I imagine the necessary vigilance of public opinion a suffi-

What men of straw in the rostra, pronouncing fiats on the immortal writings of the age; what guessers at the difference between a straight line and a curve, deciding upon the highest questions of art; what stop-watch gazers lecturing on the drama; what disappointed novelists, writhing poets, saleless historians, senseless essayists, wreaking their wrath on a lucky rival; what Damons heaping impartial eulogia on their scribbling Pythias; what presumption, what falsehood, what igno-

cient preventive of the influence complained of. The danger to which the public are exposed is more latent; the influence of acquaintance is far greater and more difficult to guard against than that of booksellers. On looking over certain Reviews, we shall find instances in which they have puffed most unduly; but it is more frequently the work of a contributor than the publication of the bookseller who promulges the Review. The job is of a more secret character than that which a title-page can betray. It is surprising indeed to see how readily the slightest and most inferior works of a contributor to one of the Quarterlies obtain a review, while those of a stranger, however important or popular, are either entirely overlooked or unnoticed, until the favour of the public absolutely forces them on the reluctant journal. It often happens that a successful writer has been most elaborately reviewed in all the other periodicals of the civilized world, and his name has become familiar to the ears of literary men throughout the globe, before the Quarterly Reviews of this country bestow the slightest notice upon him, or condescend even to acknowledge an acquaintance with his very existence. This is a wretched rance, what deceit! what malice in censure, what dishonesty in praise! Such a revelation would be worthy a Quevedo to describe!

But this would not be the sole benefit the public would derive from the authority of divulged names. They would not only know the motives of reviewers, but their capacities also; they would see if the critic were able to judge honestly, as well as willing. And this upon many intricate matters; some relating to the arts, others to the sciences; on which the public in general cannot judge for themselves, but may be easily misled by superficial notions,

effect of influence, for it attempts to create a monopoly of literature; nor is that all—it makes the judges and the judged one body, and a Quarterly Review a mere confederacy of writers united for the purpose of praising each other at all opportunities, and glancing indifferently towards the public when the greater duties of self-applause allow them leisure for the exertion. Great men contribute to these journals, and are praised—nothing more just!—but *little* men contribute also: and the jackal has his share of the bones as well as the lion. It is obvious, that if Reviews were not written anonymously, the public could not be thus cheated. If contributors put their names to their articles, they could not go on scratching each other at so indecent a rate; there would be an end to the antic system of these literary *simiæ*, who, sitting aloft on the tree of criticism, first take care to stuff themselves with the best of the fruit, and then, with the languid justice of satiety, chuck the refuse on the gazers below!

and think that the unknown author must be a great authority;—this, I say, in such cases would be an incalculable advantage, and would take the public at once out of the hands of a thousand invisible pretenders and impostors.

An argument has been adduced in favour of anonymous criticism so truly absurd, that it would not be worth alluding to, were it not so often alleged, and so often suffered to escape unridiculed. It is this: that the critic can thus take certain liberties with the author with impunity; that he may be witty or severe, without the penalty of being shot. Now, of what nature is that criticism which would draw down the author's cartel of war upon the critic?—it is not an age for duels on light offences and vague grounds. An author would be laughed at from one end of the kingdom to the other, for calling out a man for merely abusing his book; for saying that he wrote bad grammar, and was a wretched poet: if the author *were* such a fool as, on mere literary ground, to challenge a critic, the critic would scarcely be such a fool as to go out with him. " Ay," says the critic, " if I only abuse his book; but what if I abuse his person? I may censure his work safely— but supposing I want to insinuate something against his character?" True, now we under-

stand each other ; that is indeed the question.
I turn round at once from you, sir, the critic—
I appeal to the public. I ask them where is
the benefit, what the advantage of attacking a
man's person, not his book—his character, not
his composition ? Is criticism to be the act of
personal vituperation ? then, in God's name,
let us send to Billingsgate for our reviewers,
and have something racy and idiomatic at least
in the way of slang. What purpose salutary to
literature is served by hearing that Hazlitt had
pimples on his face ? How are poor Byron's
errors amended, by filthily groping among the
details of his private life—by the insinuations
and the misconstructions—by the muttered slanders—by the broad falsehoods, which filled the
anonymous channels of the press ? Was it not
this system of espionage more than any other
cause which darkened with gloomy suspicion
that mind, originally so noble ? Was not the
stinging of the lip the result of the stung heart ?
Slandered by others, his irritable mind retali-
ated by slander in return ; the openness visible
in his early character hardened into insincerity,
the constant product of suspicion ; and instead
of correcting the author, this species of criticism
contributed to deprave the man.

What did the public gain by this result of

the convenience of open speaking from invisible tongues?—nothing. But why, my dear sir, (you who have studied the literary character so deeply, and portrayed so well the calamities of authors, can perhaps tell me)—why is the poor author to be singled out from the herd of men (whom he seeks to delight or to instruct) for the sole purpose of torture? Is his nature so much less sensitive and gentle than that of others, that the utmost ingenuity is necessary to wound him? Or why is a system to be invented and encouraged, for the sole sake of persecuting him with the bitterest rancour and the most perfect impunity? Why are the rancour and the impunity to be modestly alleged as the main advantages of the system? Why are all the checks and decencies which moderate the severity of the world's censure upon its other victims, to be removed from censure upon him? Why is he to be thrust out of the pale of ordinary self-defence?—and the decorum and the fear of consequences which make the intercourse of mankind urbane and humanized, to be denied to one, whose very vanity can only be fed — whose very interests can only be promoted, by increasing the pleasures of the society which exiles him from its commonest protection—yes! by furthering the civilization which rejects him from its safe-guards?

It is not very easy, perhaps, to answer these questions; and I think, sir, that even your in-genuity can hardly discover the justice of an in-vention which visits with all the most elaborate and recondite severities that could be exercised against the enemy of his kind, the unfortunate victim who aspires to be their friend. Shak-speare has spoken of detraction as less excusable than theft; but there is a yet nobler fancy among certain uncivilized tribes, viz., that slander is a greater moral offence than even murder itself; for, say they, with an admirable shrewdness of distinction, " when you take a man's life, you take only what he *must*, at one time or an other, have lost; but when you take a man's reputation, you take that which he might otherwise have retained for ever: nay, what is yet more important, your offence in the one is bounded and definite—murder cannot travel beyond the grave—the deed imposes at once a boundary to its own effects; but in slan-der, the tomb itself does not limit the malice of your wrong—your lie may pass onward to pos-terity, and continue, generation after genera-tion, to blacken the memory of your victim."

The people of the Sandwich Islands murder-
ed Captain Cook, but they pay his memory the
highest honours which their customs acknowledge ; they retain his bones (those returned
were supposititious) which are considered sacred, and the priest thanks the gods for having
sent them so great a man. Are you surprised
at this seeming inconsistency ? Alas ! it is the
manner in which we treat the great ! We
murder them by the weapons of calumny and
persecution, and then we declare the relics of
our victim to be sacred !

But there is a third ground for deeming the
preservation of the anonymous advantageous in
periodicals ; namely, that there may be opinions
you wish to give to the world upon public
events or public characters, which private
checks of circumstance or timidity may induce
you to withhold from the world, if the publication of your name be indispensably linked
with that of your opinions.

Now if, from what I have said, it is plain the
anonymous *system* is wrong ; then the utmost
use you can make of this argument would only
prove that there are occasional exceptions to
the justness of this rule ; and this I grant
readily and at once. He is but a quack who
pretends that a general rule excludes all ex-

ceptions; and how few are the exceptions to *this* rule; how few the persons upon whom the checks alluded to legitimately operate! I leave to them the right of availing themselves of the skreen they consider necessary;—there will always be channels and opportunities enough for them to consult the anonymous, supposing that it were accordant with the *general* system of periodicals to give the public the names of their contributors.*

I have elsewhere, but more cursorily, put forth my opinions with regard to the customary

* It is also obvious that the arguments I have adduced in favour of the latter plan, do not apply to authors publishing separate works, more especially fiction, as in the instance of Sir Walter Scott and his novels: there, no one is injured by the affectation of concealment—there is no third party (no party attacked or defended) between the author and the public: I speak solely of the periodical press, which is the most influential department of the press, and how it may be most honest and most efficient towards the real interests of the community.

Consequently the reader will remark in any reply that may be put forth to these opinions, first—that it will be no answer to the justice of the rule I assert, to enumerate the exceptions I allow: secondly—that it will be no answer to my proposition relating to the periodical press to refer to the advantages of the anonymous to authors whose writings do not come under that department. With this I leave it to the People, deeply interested in the matter, to see that I am answered, not misinterpreted.

use of the anonymous in periodicals : they have
met with but little favour from periodical writers, who have continued to reiterate the old
arguments which I had already answered, rather
than attacked my replies.  In fact, journalists,
misled by some vague notions of the convenience of a plan so long adopted and so seldom
questioned, contend against a change which
would be of the most incalculable advantage to
themselves and their profession.  It is in vain
to hope that you can make the press so noble a
profession as it ought to be in the eyes of men,
as long as it can be associated in the public
mind with every species of political apostasy
and personal slander; it is in vain to hope that
the many honourable exceptions will do more
than win favour for themselves; they cannot
exalt the character of the class.  Interested as
the aristocracy are against the moral authority
of the press, and jealous as they are of its
power, they at present endeavour to render
odious the general effects of the machine, by
sneering down far below their legitimate grade
the station and respectability of the operatives.
It is in vain to deny that a newspaper-writer,
who, by his talents and the channel to which
they are applied, exerts a far greater influence
on public affairs than almost any peer in the

realm, is only of importance so long as he is in the back parlour of the printing-house; in society he not only runs the risk of being confounded with all the misdemeanours, past and present, of the journal he has contributed to purify or exalt, but he is associated with the general fear of *espionage* and feeling of insecurity which the custom of anonymous writing necessarily produces : men cannot avoid looking upon him as one who has the power of stabbing them in the dark — and the libels — the lies— the base and filthy turpitude of certain of the Sunday papers, have an effect of casting upon all newspaper writers a suspicion, from which not only the honourable, but the able* among them are utterly free—as at Venice,

---

* For to the honour of literature be it said, that the libellous Sunday papers are rarely supported by any literary men ; they are conducted chiefly by broken-down sharpers, *ci-devant* markers at gambling-houses, and the very worst description of uneducated blackguards. The only way, by the by, to check these gentlemen in their career of slander, is to be found in the first convenient opportunity of inflicting upon them that personal chastisement which is the perquisite of bullies.—Pooh ! you say, they are not worthy the punishment. Pardon me, they are not worth the denying ourselves the luxury of inflicting it. You should wait, but never miss, the convenient opportunity. In the spirit of Dr. Johnson's criticism on the Hebrides, " they are worth seeing," (said he,) " but not worth going to see," these gentlemen are worth kicking, but not worth *going* to kick.

every member of the secret council, however
humane and noble, received some portion of the
odium and the fear which attached to the practice of unwitnessed punishment and mysterious
assassination.  In short, the unhappy practice
of the anonymous, is the only reason why the
man of political power is not also the man of
social rank.  It is a practice which favours the
ignorant at the expense of the wise, and skreens
the malignant by confounding them with the
honest ;  a practice by which talent is made obscure that folly may not be detected, and the
disgrace of vice may be hidden beneath the
customs which degrade honour.

In a Spanish novel, a cavalier and a swindler
meet one another.

" Pray, sir, may I ask, why you walk with a
cloak ?" says the swindler.

" Because I do not wish to be known for
what I am," answers the gentleman.   " Let me
ask you the same question."

" Because I wish to be taken for *you*,"
answered the swindler drily.

The custom of honest men is often the shelter
of rogues.

It is quite clear that if every able writer
affixed his name to his contributions to news-

papers, the importance of his influence would soon attach to himself—

———— " Nec Phœbo gratior ulla est
Quàm sibi quæ Vari præscripsit pagina nomen.

He would no longer be confused with a herd— he would become marked and individualized— a public man as well as a public writer : he would exalt his profession as himself—the consideration accorded to him would, if he produced the same effect on his age, be the same as to a poet, philosopher, or a statesman, and now when an entrance into public life may be the result of popular esteem, it may be the readiest way of rendering men of principle and information personally known to the country, and of transferring the knowledge, which, in order to be efficient public writers, they must possess on public affairs, to that active career in which it may be the most serviceable to the country, and the most tempting to men of great acquirements and genius. Thus the profession of the Press would naturally attract the higher order of intellect — power would become infinitely better directed, and its agents immeasurably more honoured. These considerations sooner or later must have their due weight with those from whom alone the necessary reform can

spring—the journalists themselves. It is not
a point in which the legislature can interfere,
it must be left to a moral agency, which is the
result of conviction. I am firmly persuaded,
however opposed I may be now, that I shall
live to see (and to feel that I have contributed
to effect) the change.

Such is my hope for the future ; meanwhile
let me tell you an adventure that happened the
other day to an acquaintance of mine.

D—— is a sharp clever man, fond of studying character, and always thrusting his nose
into other people's affairs. He has wonderful
curiosity, which he dignifies by the more respectable name of "a talent for observation."
A little time ago D—— made an excursion of
pleasure to Calais. During his short but interesting voyage, he amused himself by recon-
noitring the passengers whom Providence had
placed in the same boat with himself. Scarcely
had his eye scanned the deck before it was
irresistibly attracted towards the figure of a
stranger, who sat alone, wrapped in his cloak,
and his meditations. My friend's curiosity was
instantly aroused : there was an inscrutable
dignity in the air of the stranger ; something
mysterious, moodful, and majestic. He resolved
to adventure upon satisfying the hungry appe-

tite for knowledge that had sprung up in his
breast : he approached the stranger, and, by
way of commencing with civility, offered him
the newspaper. The stranger glanced at him
for a moment, and shook his head. " I thank
you, sir, I have seen its contents already."
*The contents*—he did not say *the paper*, thought
D——, shrewdly, the words were not much,
but the air ! The stranger was evidently a
great man ; perhaps a diplomatist. My friend
made another attempt at a better acquaintance ;
but about this time the motion of the steam-
vessel began to affect the stranger—

And his soul sickened o'er the heaving wave.

Maladies of this sort are not favourable to
the ripening of acquaintance. My friend, baf-
fled and disappointed, shrunk into himself ;
and soon afterwards, amidst the tumult of
landing, he lost sight of his fellow-passenger.
Following his portmanteau with a jealous eye,
as it rolled along in a foreign wheelbarrow,
D—— came at last into the court-yard of M.
Dessin's hotel, and there, sauntering leisurely
to and fro, he beheld the mysterious stranger.
The day was warm ; it was delightful to bask
in the open air. D—— took a chair by the
kitchen door, and employed himself on the very

same newspaper that he had offered to the stranger, and which the cursed sea-winds had prevented his reading on the deck at that ease with which our national sense of comfort tells us that a newspaper ought to be read. Ever and anon, he took his eyes from the page and beheld the stranger still sauntering to and fro, stopping at times to gaze on a green britska with that paternal look of fondness which declared it to be an appropriation of his own.

The stranger was visibly impatient:—now he pulled out his watch—now he looked up to the heavens — now he whistled a tune—and now he muttered, " Those d—d Frenchmen !" A gentleman with an eager air, and a quick gait, entered the yard. You saw at once that he was a Frenchman. The eyes of the two gentlemen met ; they recognised each other. You might tell that the Englishman had been waiting for the new comer, the " *Bon jour mon cher*" of the Frenchman, the " How do you do" of the Englishman, were exchanged ; and D—— had the happiness of overhearing the following conversation :

*French Gentleman.* " I am ravished to congratulate you on the distinguished station you hold in Europe."

*English Gentleman* (bowing and blushing).

" Let me rather congratulate you on your accession to the peerage."

*French Gentleman.* " A bagatelle, sir, a mere bagatelle ; a natural compliment to my influence with the people. By the way, you of course will be a peer in the new batch that *must* be made shortly."

*English Gentleman* (with a constrained smile, a little in contempt and more in mortification). " No, Monsieur, no ; *we* don't make peers quite so easily."

*French Gentleman.* " Easily ! why have they not made Sir George —— and Mr. W— peers ? the one a mere *elegant*, the other a mere *gentilhomme de province*. You don't compare their claims with your great power and influence in Europe !"

*English Gentleman.* " Hum—hi—hum ; they were men of great birth and landed property."

*French Gentleman* (taking snuff). " Ah ! I thought you English were getting better of your aristocratic prejudices : *Virtus est sola nobilitas.*"

*English Gentleman.* " Perhaps those prejudices are *respectable.* By the way, to speak frankly, we were a little surprised in England at *your* elevation to the peerage."

*French Gentleman.* " Surprised ;—*diable !*
—why ?"

*English Gentleman.* " Hum — really — the
editor of a newspaper—ehum !—hem !"

*French Gentleman.* " Editor of a newspaper ! why, who *should* get political rank, but
those who wield political power? Your newspaper, for instance, is more formidable to a
minister than any duke. Now you know, with
us M. de Lalot, M. Thier,—de Villele, — Chateaubriand, and, in short, nearly all the great
men you can name, write for the newspapers."

*English Gentleman.* " Aha ! but do they
*own* it ?"

*French Gentleman.* " Own it ! to be sure ;
they are too proud to do so : how else do they
get their reputation ?"

*English Gentleman.* " Why, with us, if a
member of parliament sends us an article, it is
under a pledge of the strictest secrecy. As for
Lord Brougham, the bitterest accusation ever
made against him was, that he wrote for a certain newspaper.

*French Gentleman.* " And *did* Lord Brougham write for that newspaper ?"

*English Gentleman.* " Sir ; that is a delicate
question."

*French Gentleman.* " Why so reserved ? In

France the writers of our journals are as much known as if they put their names to their articles ; which indeed, they very often do."

*English Gentleman.* " But supposing a great man is known to write an article in my paper, all the other papers fall foul on him for demeaning himself : even *I*, while I write every day for it, should be very angry if the coxcombs of the clubs accused me of it to my face."

*French Gentleman* (laying his finger to his nose.) " I see, I see, you have not a pride of class with you, as we have. The nobleman with us, is proud of showing that he has power with those who address the people ; the plebeian writer is willing to receive a certain respectability from the assistance of the nobleman : thus each class gives consequence to the other. But you all write under a veil ; and such a number of blackguards take advantage of the concealment that the respectable man covets concealment as a skreen for himself. This is the reason that you have not—pardon me, Monsieur—as high a station as you ought to have ; and why you astonish me, by thinking it odd that I, who, vanity apart, can sway the minds of thousands every morning, should receive" (spoken with dignified disdain) " the trumpery honour of a peerage !"

" *Messieurs*, the dinner is served," said the *garçon;* and the two gentlemen walked into the salon, leaving D—— in a fever of agitation.

" *Garçon, garçon*," said he, under his breath, and beckoning to the waiter, " who is that English Gentleman ?"

" Meestare ————, the—vat you call him, le redacteur of—de editor of de—paper."

" Ha ! and the French gentleman ?"

" Monsieur Bertin de V——, pair de France, and editor of de *Journal des Debats*."

" Bless me !" said D——, " what a *rencontre !*"

Such is the account my friend D—— has given me of a dialogue between two great men. It is very likely that D——'s talents for observation may be eclipsed by his talent of invention ; I do not, therefore, give it you as a true anecdote. Look upon it, if you please, as an imaginary conversation, and tell me whether, supposing it *had* taken place, it would not have been exceedingly natural. You must class it among the instances of the *vraisemblable*, if you reject it from those of the *vrai*.

But the custom of the anonymous would never have so long sustained itself with us, had it not been sanctioned by the writers of the aristocracy—it is among the other benefits lite-

rature owes to them. It is a cloak more convenient to a man moving in a large society,
than to the scholar, who is mostly centred in a
small circle. The rich man has no power to
gain by a happy criticism, but he may have
much malice to gratify by a piquant assault.
Thus the aristocratic contributors to a journal
have the most insisted upon secrecy, and have
used it to write the bitterest sallies on their
friends. The unfortunate Lord Dudley dies,
and we learn that one of his best compositions
was a most truculent attack, in a Quarterly Review, upon his intimate companion—of course
he was anxious not to be known! There are
only two classes of men to whom the anonymous is really desirable. The perfidious gentleman who fears to be cut by the friends he in-
jures, and the lying blackguard who dreads to
be horsewhipped by the man he maligns.

With one more consideration I shall conclude
this chapter. I intimated at the commencement
of it, that the influence of the press was the
great antagonist principle to that of the aristocracy. This is a hacknied assertion, yet it is
pregnant with many novel speculations.

The influence of the press is the influence of
opinion ; yet, until very lately, the current opinion was decidedly aristocratic : — the class

mostly addressed by the press, is the middle class; yet, as we have seen before, it is among the middle class that the influence of the English aristocracy has spread some of its most stubborn roots.

How then has the press become the antagonist principle of the aristocratic power? In the first place, that portion of the press which *originates* opinion, has been mostly anti-aristocratic, and its reasonings, unpopular at first, have slowly gained ground. In the second place, the anonymous system, which favours all personal slander, and which, to feed the public taste, must slander distinguished, and not obscure, station, has forwarded the progress of opinion against the aristocratic body by the most distorted exaggeration of the individual vices or foibles of its members. By the mere details of vulgar gossip, a great wholesale principle of indignation at the privileged order has been at work; just as in ripening the feelings that led to the first French revolution, the tittle-tattle of antechambers did more than the works of philosophers. The frivolity and vices of the court provoked a bitterer contempt and resentment by well-coloured anecdotes of individual courtiers, than the elaborate logic of Diderot or the polished sarcasms of Voltaire. And wandering for one moment from the periodical press to our lighter fictions, it is undeniable that the novels which of late have been so eagerly read, and which profess to give a description of the life of the higher circles, have, in our own day, nauseated the public mind with the description of men without hearts, women without chastity, polish without dignity, and existence without use.

A third reason for the hostility of the political press to the aristocracy is to be found in the circumstances of those who write for it. They live more separated from sympathy with aristocratic influences than any other class: belonging, chiefly, to the middle order, they do not, like the middle order in general, have any dependence on the custom and favour of the great; literary men, they are not, like authors in general, courted as lions, who, mixing familiarly with their superiors, are either softened by unmeaning courtesies, or imbibe the veneration which rank and wealth personally approached, instil into the human mind, as circumstances at present form it. They mostly regard the great aloof and at a distance; they see their vices which are always published, and rarely the virtues or the amenities which are not known beyond the threshold. The system strikes them, unrelieved by any affection for its component parts. I have observed, with much amusement, the effect often produced on a periodical writer by being merely brought into contact with a man of considerable rank. He is charmed with his urbanity—astonished at his want of visible pride—he no longer sees the pensioned and titled apostate, but the agreeable man; and his next article becomes warped from its severity in despite of himself. One of the bitterest assail‑ants of Lord Eldon, having occasion to wait on that nobleman, was so impressed with the mild and kindly bearing of the man he had been attacking, that he laid it down as a rule never afterwards to say a syllable against him. So shackled do men become in great duties by the smallest conventional incidents.

But the ordinary mass of newspaper-writers being thus a peculiar and separate body, un-touched by the influence which they examine, and often galled themselves by the necessary effects of the anonymous system, have been therefore willing to co-operate to a certain and limited extent with the originators of opinion. And thus, in those crises which constantly occur in political affairs, when the popular mind, as yet undetermined, follows the first adviser in whom it has been accustomed to confide—when, in its wavering confusion, either of two opinions may be reflected, the representative portion of the press has usually taken that opinion which is the least aristocratic ; pushing the more popular, not to its full extent, but to as great an extent as was compatible with its own interest in representing rather than originating opinion. There are certain moments in all changes and transits of political power, when it makes all the difference *which* of the unsettled doubts in the public mind is expressed the first, and hastened into decision.

To these causes of the anti-aristocratic influence of the press, we must add another, broader and deeper than all. The newspaper not only discusses questions, but it gives in its varied pages, the results of systems ;—proceedings at law—convictions before magistrates—abuses in institutions—unfairness in taxation—all come before the public eye; thus, though many see not how grievances are to be redressed, all allow that the grievances exist. It is in vain to deny that the grievance is mostly on the side of the Unprivileged. No preponderating power in a state can exist for many years, without (unconsciously, perhaps,) favouring itself. We have not had an aristocratic government, without having had laws passed to its own advantage—without seeing the spirit of the presiding influence enter into our taxation, bias our legislature, and fix its fangs into our pension-lists; the last, though least really grievous of all—yet the most openly obnoxious to a commercial and over-burdened people. Nor must it be forgotten, that while the abuses of any system are thus made evident and glaring, the reasons for supporting that system in spite of abuses, are always philosophical and abstruse: so that the evil is glaring, the good unseen. This, then, is the strongest principle by which the press works against the aristocracy—the principle most constantly and most powerfully enforced. A plain recital affects more than reasoning, and seems more free from passion; and the Press, by revealing facts, exerts a far more irresistible, though less noisy sway, than by insisting on theories:—in the first it is the witness, in the last, the counsel.

And yet this spirit of Revelation is the greatest of all the blessings which the liberty of the press confers; it is of this which philosophers speak when they grow warm upon its praises—when wisdom loses its measured tone of approval, and reasoning itself assumes the language of declamation. As the nature of evi-

dence is the comparison of facts, so to tell us all
things on all sides is the sole process by which
we arrive at truth. From the moment an abuse
is published, we are certain that the abuse
will be removed. In the sublime language
of a great moralist, " Errors cease to be dangerous when it is permitted to contradict them ;
they are soon known to be errors ; they sink
into the Abyss of Forgetfulness, and Truth
alone swims over the vast extent of Ages."
This publicity is man's nearest approach to the
omniscience of his great Creator ; it is the
largest result of union yet known, for it is the
expression of the Universal Mind. Thus are we
enabled, knowing what *is* to be effected, to effect
according to our knowledge—for to knowledge
power is proportioned. Omnipotence is the necessary consequence of omniscience. Nor can we
contemplate without a deep emotion, what may
be the result of that great measure, which must
sooner or later be granted by the legislature, and
which, by the destruction of the stamp duty on
political periodicals, will extend to so unbounded
a circle this sublime prerogative of publicity—
of conveying principles — of expressing opinion
—of promulging fact. So soon as the first confusion that attends the sudden opening of a long
monopoly is cleared away—when it is open to

every man, rich or poor, to express the knowledge he has hoarded in his closet, or even at
his loom; when the stamp no longer confines to
a few the power of legitimate instruction ; when
all may pour their acquirements into the vast
commonwealth of knowledge — it is impossible
to calculate the ultimate results to human science, and the advancement of our race.   Some
faint conjecture may be made from a single
glance at the crowded reports of a parliamentary
committee ; works containing a vast hoard of
practical knowledge, of inestimable detail, often
collected from witnesses who otherwise would
have been dumb for ever ; works now unread,
scarce known, confined to those who want them
least, by them not rendered profitable : when
we recollect that in popular and familiar shapes
that knowledge and those details will ultimately
find a natural vent, we may form some slight
groundwork of no irrational guesses towards
the future ; when the means of knowledge
shall be open to all who read, and its expression to all who think.   Nor must we forget, that
from the mechanic, the mechanic will more easily
learn ; as it has been discovered in the Lan-
caster schools, that by boys, boys can be best
instructed.   Half the success of the pupil depends on his familiarity and sympathy with the

master. Reflections thus opened to us, expand
into hopes, not vague, not unfounded, but
which no dreams of imaginary optimism have
yet excelled. What triumph for him, who, in
that divine spirit of prophecy which foresees
in future happiness the result of present legislation, has been a disciple—a worker for the
saving truth, that enlightenment furthers amelioration—who has built the port and launched
the ship, and suffered the obstacles of nature
and the boundaries of the world to be the only
bar and limit to the commerce of the mind : he
may look forward into time, and see his own
name graven upon a thousand landmarks of the
progress of the human intellect. Such men
are, to *all* wisdom, what Bacon was only to a
part of it. It is better to allow philosophy to
be universal, than to become a philosopher.
The wreath that belongs to a fame of this order
will be woven from the best affections of mankind : its glory will be the accumulated gratitude of generations. It is said, that in the
Indian plain of Dahia, the Creator drew forth
from the loins of Adam his whole posterity :
assembled together in the size and semblance of
small ants, these pre-existent nations acknowledged God, and confessed their origin in his
power. Even so in some great and living pro-

VOL. II.

ject for the welfare of mankind—the progenitor of benefits, uncounted and unborn we may trace the seeds of its offspring even to the confines of eternity; we may pass before us, though in a dwarfed and inglorious shape, the mighty and multiplied blessings to which it shall give birth, all springing from one principle, all honouring HIM, who of that principle was the Vivifier and the Maker!

# CHAPTER II.

## LITERATURE.

Observation of a German—Great Writers and no great Works—The Poverty of our present Literature in all Departments, save the Imaginative—History—Political Composition—The Belles Lettres peculiarly barren—Remarks on the Writings of D'Israeli, Hazlitt, Charles Lamb and Southey—Causes of the Decline of the Belles Lettres, and the undiminished Eminence of fictitious Literature alone—The Revolution that has been wrought by Periodicals—The Imaginative Faculty has reflected the Philosophy of the Age—Why did Scott and Byron represent the Mind of their Generation?—The Merit of Lord Byron's earlier Poems exaggerated—Want of Grandeur in their Conception—The Merit of his Tragedies undervalued—Brief Analysis in support of these Opinions—Why did the Tragedies disappoint the World?—The Assertion that Byron wanted Variety in dramatic Character contradicted—The Cause of the public Disappointment—The Age identified itself with him *alone*—Recollections of the Sensations produced by his Death—Transition of the Intellectual Spirit of the Period from the ideal to the actual—Cause of the craving for fashionable Novels—Their Influence—Necessity of cultivating the—Imagination Present intellectual Disposition and Tendency of the Age.

" THIS is a great literary epoch with your nation," said a German to me the other day, " You have magnificent *writers* amongst you at this day, their names are known all over Europe ; but (putting the poets out of the question) where, to ask a simple question, are their writings ?—which are the great prose works of your contemporaries that you recommend mc

to read ?   What, especially, are the recent masterpieces in criticism and the *belles lettres ?*"

This question, and the lame answer that I
confess I gave to it, set me upon considering
why we had undoubtedly at this day many
great writers in the Humane Letters, and yet
very few great books.   For the last twenty years
the intellectual faculties have been in full foliage,
but have borne no fruit, save on one tree alone;
the remarkable fertility of which forcibly contrasts the barrenness of the rest, and may be
considered among the most startling of the
literary phenomena of the times—I mean the
faculty of the Imagination.   I am asked for the
great books we have produced during the last
twenty years, and my memory instantly reverts
to the *chef-d'œuvres* of poets and writers of
fiction.   The works of Byron, Wordsworth,
Scott, Moore, Shelley, Campbell, rush at once
to my tongue: nay, I should refer to later
writers in imaginative literature, whose celebrity
is, as yet, unmellowed, and whose influence
limited, long ere the contemporary works of a
graver nature would force themselves on my
recollection: debar me the imaginative writings,
and I could more easily close my catalogue of
great works than begin it.

In imaginative literature, then, we are peculiarly rich, in the graver letters we are as singularly barren.

In History we have surely not even secondary names; we have commentators on history, rather than historians: and the general dimness of the atmosphere may be at once acknowledged, when we point as luminaries to a * * * * * * and a * * * * †

In Moral Philosophy, a subject which I shall reserve for a separate chapter, the reputation of one or two high names does not detract from the general sterility. Few indeed are the works in this noble department of knowledge, that have been, if published, *made known to the public* for a period inconceivably long, when we consider that we live in an age when the jargon of moral philosophy is so popularly affected.

In that part of political literature which does not embrace political economy, we are also without any great works: but yet, singularly enough,

† But if we cannot boast of men capable of grasping the events of past ages, we have, at least, one, who in the spirit of ancient history has painted with classic colours the scenes in which he himself was an actor; and has left to posterity the records of a great war, written with the philosophy of Polybius, and more than the eloquence, if less than the simplicity, of Cæsar. I need scarcely add, that I refer to the *History of the Peninsular War*, by Colonel Napier.

not without many perhaps unequalled writers—
Southey, Wilson, Cobbett, Sidney Smith, the
profound and vigorous editor of the *Examiner*,
the original and humorous author of the *Corn Law
Catechism*, and many others whom I can name,
(but that almost every influential Journal betrays
the eminent talent that supports it), are men who
have developed some of the highest powers of
composition, in a series of writings intended only
for the hour.    In miscellaneous literature, or
what is commonly termed the *belles lettres*, we
have not very remarkably enriched the collection bequeathed to us by the Johnsonian era.
The name of one writer I cannot, however, help
singling from the rest, as that of the most elegant gossip upon the learned letters, not only
of his time, but, perhaps, his country ; and I
select it the more gladly, because popular as
he is, I do not think he has ever obtained from
criticism a fair acknowledgment of the eminent
station he is entitled to claim.    The reader has
already discovered that I speak of yourself, the
author of *The Curiosities of Literature*, *The
Calamities of Authors*, and, above all, the
*Essay upon the Literary Character*.    In the
two first of these works you have seemed to me
to be to literature what Horace Walpole was to
a court ;—drawing from minutiæ, which you

are too wise to deem frivolities, the most novel deductions, and the most graceful truths; and seeming to gossip, where in reality you philosophize. But you have that which Horace Walpole never possessed—that which is necessary to the court of Letters, but forbidden to the Court of Kings: a deep and tender vein of sentiment runs, at no unfrequent times, through your charming lucubrations; and I might instance, as one of the most touching, yet unexaggerated conceptions of human character, that even a novelist ever formed, the beautiful *Essay upon Shenstone.* That, indeed, which particularly distinguishes your writings, is your marvellous and keen sympathy with the literary character in all its intricate mazes and multiplied varieties of colour. You identify yourself wholly with the persons on whom you speculate; you enter into their heart, their mind, their caprices, their habits, and their eccentricities; and this quality, so rare even in a dramatist, is entirely new in an essayist. I know of no other lucubrator who possesses it : with a subtile versatility you glide from one character to another, and by examination re-create ;—drawing from research all those new views and bold deductions which the poet borrows from imagination. The gallant and crafty Raleigh, the melancholy

Shenstone, the antiquarian Oldys—each how
different, each how profoundly analyzed, each
how peculiarly the author's own! Even of the
least and lowest, you say something new.
Your art is like that which Fontaine would
attribute to a more vulgar mastery:

——Un roi, prudent et sage,
De ses moindres sujets fait tirer quelque usage.

But the finest of all your works, to my
mind, is the *Essay on the Literary Character;*
a book, which he who has once read, ever re-
curs to with delight: it is one of those rare
works, in which every part is adorned, yet subordinate to the whole—in which every page dis-
plays a beauty, and none an impertinence.

You recollect the vigorous assault made at
one time against a peculiar school of writers;
years have passed, and on looking back over the
additions those years have brought to our *belles
lettres,* the authors of that calumniated school
immediately occur to us. The first of these writers is Mr. Hazlitt, a man of a nervous and original mind, of great powers of expression, of a
cool reason, of a warm imagination, of imperfect
learning, and of capricious and unsettled taste.
The chief fault of his essays is, that they are
vague and desultory; they leave no clear con-

clusion on the mind; they are a series of brilliant observations, without a result. If you are wiser when you have concluded one of them, it seems as if you were made so by accident: some aphorism, half an impertinence, in the middle of the essay, has struck on the truth, which the peroration, probably, will again carefully wrap in obscurity. He has aspired to be the universal critic; he has commented on art and letters, philosophy, manners, and men: in regard to the last, for my own part, I would esteem him a far more questionable authority than upon the rest; for he is more occupied in saying shrewd things of character, than in giving you the character itself. He wanted, perhaps, a various and actual experience of mankind in all its grades; and if he had the sympathy which compensates for experience, it was not a catholic sympathy, it was bestowed on particular tenets and their professors, and was erring, because it was sectarian. But in letters and in art, prejudice blinds less than it does in character; and in these the metaphysical bias of his mind renders him often profound, and always ingenious; while the constant play of his fancy redeems and brightens even the occasional inaccuracy of his taste.

Mr. Liegh Hunt's Indicator contains some of the most delicate and subtle criticisms in the language. His kindly and cheerful sympathy with Nature—his perception of the minuter and more latent sources of the beautiful—spread an irresistible charm over his compositions,—but he has not as yet done full justice to himself in his prose writings, and must rest his main reputation upon those exquisite poems which the age is beginning to appreciate.

*The Essays of Elia,* in considering the recent additions to our *belles lettres,* cannot be passed over in silence. Their beauty is in their delicacy of sentiment. Since Addison, no writer has displayed an equal refinement of humour ; and if no single one of Mr. Lamb's conceptions equals the elaborate painting of Sir Roger de Coverley, yet his range of character is more extensive than Addison's, and in his humour there is a deeper pathos. His compositions are so perfectly elaborate, and so minutely finished, that they partake rather of the character of poetry than of prose ; they are as perfect in their way as the Odes of Horace, and at times, as when commencing his invocation to " the Shade of Elliston " he breaks forth with

" Joyousest of once-embodied spirits, whither at length hast thou flown ? " &c.

we might almost fancy that he had set Horace before him as a model.

But the most various, scholastic, and accomplished of such of our literary contemporaries as have written works as well as articles, and prose as well as poetry—is, incontestably, Dr. Southey. "The Life of Nelson" is acknowledged to be the best biography of the day· "The Life of Wesley" and "The Book of the Church," however adulterated by certain prepossessions and prejudices, are, as mere compositions, characterized by an equal simplicity and richness of style,—an equal dignity and an equal ease. No writer blends more happily the academical graces of the style of the last century, with the popular vigour of that which distinguishes the present. His Colloquies are, I suspect, the work on which he chiefly prides himself, but they do not seem to me to contain the best characteristics of his genius. The work is overloaded with quotation and allusion, and, like Tarpeia, seems crushed beneath the weight of its ornaments; it wants the great charm of that simple verve which is so peculiarly Southeian. Were I to do justice to Southey's cast of mind—to analyse its properties and explain its apparent contradictions, I should fill the two volumes of this work with

Southey alone.    Suffice it *now* (another occasion
to do him ampler justice may occur elsewhere,)
to make two remarks in answer to the common
charges against this accomplished writer.    He
is alleged to be grossly inconsistent in politics,
and wholly unphilosophical in morals.    I hold
both these charges to spring from the coarse in-
justice of party.    If ever a man wrote a complete vindication of himself—that vindication is
to be found in Southey's celebrated Letter to a
certain Member of Parliament ; the triumphant
dignity with which he puts aside each successive
aspersion — the clearness with which, in that
Letter, his bright integrity shines out through
all the mists amidst which it voluntarily passes,
no dispassionate man can mark and not admire.
But he is not philosophical?—No,—rather say
he is not logical ; his philosophy is large and
learned, but it is founded on hypothesis, and
is poetical not metaphysical.    What I shall
afterwards say of Wordsworth would be equally
applicable to Southey, had the last been less
passionate and less of a political partisan.

It would be no unpleasant task to pursue yet
farther the line of individual criticism ; but in
a work of this nature, single instances of literary
merit are only cited as illustrations of a particular state of letters ; and the mention of

authors must be regarded merely in the same light as quotations from books, in which some compliment is indeed rendered to the passage quoted, but assuredly without disrespect to those which do not recur so easily to our memory, or which seem less apposite to our purpose.

Still, recurring to my first remark, we cannot but feel impressed, while adducing some names in the non-inventive classes of literature, with the paucity of those that remain. It is a great literary age—we have great literary men—but where are their works? a moment's reflection gives us a reply to the question; we must seek them not in detached and avowed and standard publications, but in periodical miscellanies. It is in these journals that the most eminent of our recent men of letters, have chiefly obtained their renown—it is here that we find the sparkling and sarcastic Jeffrey—the incomparable humour and transparent logic of Sidney Smith—the rich and glowing criticism of Wilson — the nervous vigour and brilliant imagination of Macauley, (who, if he had not been among the greatest of English orators, would have been among the most commanding of English authors;) it is in periodicals that many of the most beautiful evidences of Southey's rich taste and antique stateliness of mind are to be sought, and that the admirable editor of *The Examiner* has embodied the benevolence of Bentham in the wit of Courier. Nay, even a main portion of the essays, which, now collected in a separate shape,* have become a permanent addition to our literature, first appeared amidst a crowd of articles of fugitive interest in the journals of the day, and owe to the accident of republication their claims to the attention of posterity. From this singular circumstance, as the fittest fact whereon to build our deductions, we may commence our survey of the general Intellectual Spirit of the Time.

The revolution that has been effected by Periodical Literature, is, like all revolutions, the result of no immediate causes; it commenced so far back as the reign of Anne. The success of the *Tatler* and *Spectator* opened a new field to the emulation of literary men,† and in the natural sympathy between literature and politics, the same channels into which the one was directed afforded equal temptation to the other;

---

* Elia, many of the Essays of Hazlitt, &c.

† The " Review " of De Foe, commencing in 1704 and continued till 1713, embraced not only matters on politics and trade, but also what he termed a *scandal club*, which treating on poetry, criticism, &c. contained the probable germ of the *Tatler* and *Spectator*.

men of the highest intellect and rank were delighted to resort to a constant and frequent
means of addressing the public; the political
opinions of Addison, Steele, Swift, Boling-
broke, and the fitful ambition of Wharton himself, found vent in periodical composition. The
fashion once set, its advantages were too obvious for it not to continue; and thus the examples of Chesterfield and Pulteney, of Johnson,
Goldsmith, and Mackenzie, sustained the dignity of this species of writing so unpretending
in its outward appearance, and demanding
therefore so much excellence to preserve its importance. The fame acquired by periodical
essays gave consequence and weight to periodical miscellanies—criticism became a vocation
as books multiplied. The *Journal des Sçavans*
of the French begat imitators in England; similar journals rose and increased in number and
influence, and the reviewers soon grew a corpo-
rate body and a formidable tribunal. The abuses
consequent, as we have shown, on an anonymous system, began to be early apparent in
these periodicals, which were generally feeble
in proportion to their bulk, and of the less
value according to their greater ostentation.
The public sickened of *The Monthly Review*,
and the *Edinburgh Quarterly* arose. From the

appearance of this latter work, which was the crown and apex of periodical reviews, commences the deterioration of our standard literature;—and the dimness and scantiness of isolated works on politics, criticism, and the *belles lettres*, may be found exactly in proportion to the brilliancy of this new focus, and the rapidity with which it attracted to itself the talent and knowledge of the time. The effect which this work produced, its showy and philosophical tone of criticism, the mystery that attached to it, the excellence of its composition, soon made it an honour to be ranked among its contributors. The length of time intervening between the publication of its numbers was favourable to the habits and taste of the more elaborate and scholastic order of writers; what otherwise they would have published in a volume, they willingly condensed into an essay; and found for the first time in miscellaneous writings, that with a less risk of failure than in an isolated publication, they obtained, for the hour at least, an equal reputation. They enjoyed indeed a double sort of fame, for the article not only obtained praise for its own merit, but caught no feeble reflection from the general esteem conferred upon the Miscellany itself; add to this the high terms of pecuniary remuneration, till then unknown in periodicals, so tempting to the immediate wants of the younger order of writers, by which an author was sure of obtaining for an essay in the *belles lettres* a sum almost equal to that which he would have gleaned from a respectable degree of success if the essay had been separately given to the world; and this by a mode of publication which saved him from all the chances of loss, and the dread of responsibility ;—the certain anxiety, the probable mortification. In a few years the *Quarterly Review* divided the public with the *Edinburgh*, and the opportunities afforded to the best writers of the day to express, periodically, their opinions, were thus doubled. The consequence was unavoidable; instead of writing volumes authors began pretty generally to write articles, and a literary excrescence monopolized the nourishment that should have extended to the whole body : hence talent, however great ; taste, however exquisite ; knowledge, however enlarged, were directed to fugitive purposes. Literary works, in the magnificent thought of Bacon, are the Ships of Time ; precious was the cargo wasted upon vessels which sunk for ever in a three-months' voyage ! What might not Jeffrey and Sidney Smith, in the vigour of their age, have produced as authors, if they had been less industrious as reviewers. The evil increased by degrees; the profoundest writers began to perceive that the period allotted to the duration of an article was scarcely sufficient inducement to extensive and exhausting labour; (even in a quarterly review the brilliant article dazzled more than the deep: for true wisdom requires time for appreciation,) and, though still continuing the mode of publication which proffered so many conveniences, they became less elaborate in their reasonings and less accurate in their facts.

Thus, by a natural reaction, a temporary form of publication produced a bias to a superficial order of composition; and, while intellectual labour was still attracted towards one quarter, it was deteriorated, as monopolies are wont to be, by the effects of monopoly itself. But, happily, there was one faculty of genius which these miscellanies could not materially attract, and that was the IMAGINATIVE. The poet and the novelist had no temptation to fritter away their conceptions in the grave and scholastic pages of the Quarterly Journals; they were still compelled, if they exceeded the slender limits allotted to them in magazines, to put forth separate works; to incur individual responsibility; to appeal to Time, as their tribunal;

to meditate — to prepare — to perfect. Hence
one principal reason, among others, why the
Imaginative Literature of the day has been so
much more widely and successfully cultivated
than any other branch of intellectual exertion.
The best writers in other branches write the
reviews, and leave only the inferior ones to
write the books.

The Imaginative Faculty thus left to its natural and matured tendencies, we may conceive
that the spirit and agitation of the age exercised
upon the efforts it produced the most direct
and permanent influence. And it is in the
poetry and the poetic prose of our time that we
are chiefly to seek for that sympathy which
always exists between the intellectual and the
social changes in the prevalent character and
sentiment of a People.

There is a certain period of civilization, ere
yet men have begun to disconnect the principles
to be applied to future changes from a vague
reference to former precedents; when amend-
ment is not orthodox, if considered a novelty;
and an improvement is only imagined a return
to some ancient and dormant excellence. At
that period all are willing to listen with reverential interest to every detail of the Past; the
customs of their ancestors have for them a

superstitious attraction, and even the spirit of innovation is content to feed itself from the devotion to antiquity.   It was at this precise period that the genius of Walter Scott brought into vivid portraiture the very images to which Inquiry was willing to recur,  satisfied the half unconscious desire of the age, and represented its scarcely expressed opinion.   At that period, too, a distaste to the literature immediately preceding the time had grown up ;  a vague feeling that our poetry, become frigid and tame by echoed gallicisms, required some return to the national and more primitive tone.   Percy's *Ballads* had produced a latent suspicion of the value of re-working forgotten mines :  and, above all, perhaps, purer and deeper notions of Shakspeare had succeeded the vulgar criticism that had long depreciated his greatest merits ;  he had become studied, as well as admired ; an affection had grown up not only for the creations of his poetry, but the stately and antique language in which they were clothed.   These feelings in the popular mind, which was in that state when both Poetry and Philosophy were disposed to look favourably on any able and deliberate recurrence to the manners and the spirit of a past age, Sir Walter Scott was the first vividly and popularly to represent ; and, therefore, it is to his pages that the wise historian will look not only for an epoch in poetical literature, but the reflection of the moral sentiment of an age. The prose of that great author is but a continuation of the effect produced by his verse, only cast in a more familiar mould, and adapted to a wider range;—a reverberation of the same tone, carrying the sound to a greater distance.

A yet more deep and enduring sentiment of the time was a few years afterwards embodied by the dark and meditative genius of Byron; but I apprehend that Criticism, amidst all the inquiries it directed towards the causes of the sensation produced by that poet, did not give sufficient importance to those in reality the most effective.*

Let us consider:—

In the earlier portion of this work, in attempt-

* I do not here stop to trace the manner in which the genius of Scott or Byron was formed by the writings of less popular authors: Wordsworth and Coleridge assisted greatly towards the ripening of those feelings which produced the Lay of the Last Minstrel and Childe Harold:—my present object is, however, merely to show the sentiment of the age as embodied in the most *popular* and acknowledged shapes. If my limits allowed me to go somewhat more backward in the critical history of our literature, I could trace the first origin, or rather revival of our (modern) romantic poetry to an earlier founder than Coleridge, who is usually considered its parent.

ing to trace the causes operating on the National Character of the English, I ascribed to the peculiar tone and cast of our aristocracy much of that reserved and unsocial spirit which proverbially pervades all classes of our countrymen. To the same causes, combined with the ostentation of commerce, I ascribed also much of that hollowness and glitter which belong to the occupations of the great world, and that fretfulness and pride, that uneasy and dissatisfied temper, which are engendered by a variety of small social distinctions, and the eternal *vying*, and consequent mortification, which those distinctions produce. These feelings, the slow growth of centuries, became more and more developed as the effects of civilization and wealth rendered the aristocratic influences more general upon the subordinate classes. In the indolent luxuries of a court, what more natural than satiety among the great, and a proud discontent among their emulators? The peace just concluded, and the pause in continental excitement, allowed these pampered, yet not unpoetical springs of sentiment, to be more deeply and sensibly felt ; and the public, no longer compelled by War and the mighty career of Napoleon to turn their attention to the action of life, could give their sympathies undivided to the

first who should represent their thoughts. And
these very thoughts, these very sources of sentiment—this very satiety—this very discontent—
this profound and melancholy temperament, the
result of certain social systems—the first two
cantos of *Childe Harold* suddenly appeared to
represent. They touched the most sensitive
chord in the public heart—they expressed what
every one felt. The position of the author once
attracting curiosity, was found singularly correspondent with the sentiment he embodied
His rank, his supposed melancholy, even his
reputed beauty, added a natural interest to his
genius. He became the Type, the Ideal of the
state of mind he represented, and the world
willingly associated his person with his works,
because they thus seemed actually to incorporate, and in no undignified or ungraceful shape,
the principle of their own long-nursed sentiments
and most common emotions. Sir Philip Sidney
represented the popular sentiment in Elizabeth's
day —Byron that in our own. Each became
the poetry of a particular age put into action—
each, incorporated with the feelings he addressed, attracted towards himself an enthusiasm which his genius alone did not deserve.
It is in vain, therefore, that we would now coolly
criticise the merits of the first Cantos of *Childe*

*Harold*, or those Eastern Tales by which they
were succeeded, and in which another sentiment
of the age was addressed, namely, that craving
for adventure and wild incident which the habit
of watching for many years the events of a por-
tentous War, and the meteoric career of the
modern Alexander, naturally engendered. We
may wonder, when we now return to those
poems, at our early admiration at their supposed philosophy of tone and grandeur of
thought. In order to judge them fairly, we
must recall the feelings they addressed. With
nations, as with individuals, it is necessary to
return to past emotions in order to judge of the
merits of past appeals to them. We attributed
truth and depth to Lord Byron's poetry in proportion as it expressed our own thoughts; just
as in the affairs of life, or in the speeches of orators, we esteem those men the most sensible who
agree the most with ourselves—embellishing and
exalting only (not controverting) our own impressions. And in tracing the career of this
remarkable poet, we may find that he became
less and less popular in proportion, not as
his genius waned, but as he addressed more
feebly the prevalent sentiment of his times:
for I suspect that future critics will agree that
there is in his tragedies, which were never po-

pular, a far higher order of genius than in his
Eastern Tales or the *first* two cantos of *Childe
Harold*. The highest order of poetical genius
is usually evinced by the conception rather than
the execution; and this often makes the main
difference between Melodrame and Tragedy.
There is in the early poems of Lord Byron
scarcely any clear conception at all; there is
no harmonious plan, comprising one great, consistent, systematic whole; no epic of events art-
fully wrought, progressing through a rich variety of character, and through the struggles of
contending passions, to one mighty and inevitable end. If we take the most elaborate and
most admired of his tales, *The Corsair*, we shall
recognize in its conception an evident want of
elevation. A pirate taken prisoner—released by
a favourite of the harem—escaping—and finding his mistress dead; there is surely nothing
beyond melodrame in the design of this story,
nor do the incidents evince any great fertility
of invention to counterbalance the want of
greatness in the conception. In this too, as in
all his tales, though full of passion—and this is
worth considering, since it is for his delineations of passion that the vulgar laud him—we
may observe that he describes a passion, not
the *struggles* of passions. But it is in the last

VOL. II.

that a master is displayed: it is contending emotions, not the prevalence of one emotion, that call forth all the subtle comprehension, or deep research, or giant grasp of man's intricate nature, in which consists the highest order of that poetic genius which works out its result by character and fiction. Thus the struggles of Medea are more dread than the determination ; the conflicting passions of Dido evince the most triumphant effect of Virgil's skill ;—to describe a murder is the daily task of the melodramatist —the irresolution, the horror, the *struggle* of Macbeth, belong to Shakspeare alone.   When Byron's heroes commit a crime, they march at once to it : we see not the pause—the self-coun-sel—the agony settling into resolve; he enters not into that delicate and subtle analysis of human motives which excites so absorbing a dread, and demands so exquisite a skill.   Had Shakspeare conceived a Gulnare, he would probably have presented to us in terrible detail her pause over the couch of her sleeping lord : we should have seen the woman's weakness contesting with the bloody purpose ; she would have remembered, though even with loathing, that on the breast she was about to strike, her head had been pil-lowed ;—she would have turned aside—shrunk from her design—again raised the dagger : you

would have heard the sleeping man breathe—
she would have quailed—and, quailing, struck!
But the death-chamber—that would have been
the scene in which, above all others, Shakspeare would have displayed himself—is barred
and locked to Byron. He gives us the crime,
and not all the wild and fearful preparation
to it. So again in Parisina:—from what opportunities of exercising his art does the poet
carefully exclude himself! With what minute,
and yet stern analysis, would Sophocles have
exhibited the contest in the breast of the adul-
teress!—the love—the honour—the grief—the
dread—the horror of the incest, and the violence
of the passion!—but Byron proceeds at once to
the guilty meeting, and the tragic history is,
as much as can be compatible with the materials, merged into the amorous fragment. If
Byron had, in his early poems, conceived the
history of Othello, he would have given us
the murder of Desdemona, but never the inter-
views with Iago. Thus, neither in the conception of the plot, nor the fertile invention of incident, nor, above all, in the dissection of passions, can the early poems of Lord Byron rank
with the higher masterpieces of Poetical Art.

But at a later period of his life more exalted
and thoughtful notions of his calling were re-

vealed to him, and I imagine that his acquaintance with Shelley induced him to devote his
meditative and brooding mind to those metaphysical inquiries into the motives and actions
of men which lead to deep and hidden sources
of character, and a more entire comprehension
of the science of poetical analysis.

Hence his tragedies evince a much higher
order of conception, and a much greater mastery
in art than his more celebrated poems. What
more pure or more lofty than his character of
Angiolina, in *The Doge of Venice!* I know not
in the circle of Shakspeare's women, one more
true, not only to nature—that is a slight merit
—but to the highest and rarest order of nature.
Let us pause here for one moment—we are in
no hacknied ground. The character has never
yet been fully understood. An insulting libel
on the virtue of Angiolina, by Steno, a young
patrician, is inscribed on the ducal throne;
the Doge demands the head of the libeller;—
the Tribunal of the Forty award *a month's im-
prisonment!* What are Angiolina's feelings on
the first insult—let her speak for herself:

> " I heed it not
> For the rash scorner's falsehood in itself,
> But for the effect, the deadly deep mpression
> Which it has made upon Faliero's soul.

*   *   *   *   *

MARIANNA.

Assuredly
The Doge can not suspect you?

ANGIOLINA.

*Suspect me!—*
*Why Steno dared not.—*
\*    \*    \*    \*    \*

MARIANNA.

'Twere fit
He should be punish'd grievously.

ANGIOLINA.

He is so.

MARIANNA.

What! is the sentence pass'd?—is he condemn'd?

ANGIOLINA.

I know not that—*but he has been detected.*
\*    \*    \*    \*    \*

MARIANNA.

Some sacrifice is due to slander'd virtue.

ANGIOLINA.

Why, what is virtue if it needs a victim?
Or if it must depend upon men's words?
The dying Roman said, " 'twas but a name:"
It were indeed no more, if human breath
Could make or mar it.——

What deep comprehension of the dignity of
virtue! Angiolina will not even conceive that
she *can* be suspected; or, that an insult upon
her should need other justice than the indignation of opinion! Marianna subsequently asks,
if, when Angiolina gave her hand to the Doge,

With this strange disproportion in your years,
And, let me add, disparity of tempers,

she yet loved her father's friend—her spouse :
If,

——Previous to this marriage, had your heart
Ne'er beat for any of the noble youth,
Such as in years had been more meet to match
Beauty like yours? or since have you ne'er seen
One, who, if your fair hand were still to give,
Might now pretend to Loredano's daughter?

ANGIOLINA.

I answer'd your *first* question when I said
I married.

MARIANNA.

And the second?

ANGIOLINA.

*Needs no answer !*

Is not this conception even equal to that of
" the gentle lady wedded to the Moor ?"   The
same pure, serene, tender, yet scarce impassioned heart, that loves the abstract, not the
actual ; that, like Plato, incorporates virtue in
a visible shape, and then allows it no rival.;—
yet this lofty and proud woman has no sternness in her nature ; she forgives Steno, not from
the calm haughtiness of her high chastity alone.
" Had," she says to the angry Doge,

" Oh ! had this false and flippant libeller
" Shed his young blood for his absurd lampoon,
" Ne'er from that moment could this breast have known
" A joyous hour, or dreamless slumber more."

Here the reader will note with how delicate an art the sex's tenderness and charity relieve and warm the snowy coldness of her ethereal superiority. What a union of woman's best qualities! the pride that disdains reproach, the meekness that forgives it! Nothing can be more simply grand than the whole of this character, and the history which it exalts. The old man of eighty years, wedded to the young wife; her heart never wandering, no episode of love disturbing its serene orbit, no impure or dishonouring jealousy casting its shadow upon her bright name; she moves through the dread scene, all angelic in her qualities, yet all human in the guise they assume. In his earlier years Byron would, as he intimates, have lowered and hacknied the antique dignity of this Ideal, by an imitation of the Moor's jealousy: nay, *in yet earlier years* he would, I believe, have made Angiolina guilty; he would have mingled, perhaps, more passionate interest with the stern pathos of the story; but interest of how much less elevated a cast! Who can compare the ideal of Parisina with that of Angiolina? I content myself with merely pointing out the majesty and truth with which the character of the Doge himself is conceived; his fiery and headlong wrath against the libeller, frozen

at once by the paltry sentence on his crime; and
transferred to the tribunal that adjudged it; his
ire at the insult of the libel, merged in a deeper
passion at that of the punishment; his patrician
self-scorn at his new fellowship with plebeian
conspirators; his paternal and patriarchal tenderness for Angiolina—devoid of all uxorious-
ness and doting; the tragic decorum with which
his love is invested; and the consummate and
even sublime skill, which, allowing equal scope
for passion with that manifested in Othello,
makes the passion yet more lofty and refined;
for in the Moor, the human and the sexual are,
perhaps, too strongly marked—in the Doge,
they seem utterly merged.

Again, what beautiful conception in the tale
of the *Foscari!* how original, how tender, the
love of soil in Jacopo—Greek in its outline, but
Ausonian in its colouring: you see the very patriotism natural to the sweet south—the heart

> Which never beat
> For Venice, but with such a yearning as
> The dove has for her distant nest—

the conception of this peculiar patriotism,
which is for the air, the breath of Venice;
which makes a bodily and visible mistress of
the sea-girt city; which courts torture, death,
dishonour, for one hour alone of her presence—

all this is at once thoroughly original and
deeply tragic. In vain they give him life—he
asks for liberty: in vain they give him liberty,
he asks for Venice—he cannot dissociate the
two:

> I could endure my dungeon, for 'twas Venice;
> I could support the torture, there was something
> In my native air that buoy'd my spirits up—
>
> \*     \*     \*     \*     \*
>
>         *but afar—*
> *My very soul seem'd mouldering in my bosom.*

In vain, Marina, the brave, the passionate wife,
exclaims

> This love of thine
> For an ungrateful and tyrannic soil
> Is passion, and not patriotism.—

In this truth is the originality and Euripidean
pathos of the conception. In vain she reminds
him of the " lot of millions"

> The hereditary exiles that have been.

He answers,

>         Who can number
> The hearts which broke in silence of that parting,
> Or after that departure; of that malady
> Which calls up green and native fields to view
> From the rough deep?
>
>    \*     \*     \*     \*     \*
>
> ——You call this weakness! It is strength,
> I say,—the parent of all honest feeling.
> He who loves not his country, can love nothing.

In vain again, with seemingly unanswerable logic, Marina replies,

> Obey her, then; 'tis *she* that puts thee forth.

With what sudden sinking of the heart he replies,

> Ay, there it is: 'tis like a mother's curse
> Upon my soul.

Mark, too, how wonderfully the character of the austere old father, hardened and marbled by the peculiar and unnatural systems of Venetian policy, contrasts that of the son: in both patriotism is the ruling passion; yet how differently developed!

> First at the board in this unhappy process
> Against his last and only son!—

But what glimpses reveal to you the anguish of the father! With what skill your sympathy is enlisted in his behalf; and repugnance at his severity converted into admiration of his devotion!

> MARINA.
>     What shall I say
> To Foscari from his father?

> DOGE.
>     That he obey
> The laws.

> MARINA.
>    And nothing more? Will you not see him
> Ere he depart? It may be the last time.

### DOGE.

The last!—my boy!—the last time I shall see
My last of children!  *Tell him I will come.*

The same deep and accurate knowledge of
the purest sources of effect which taught the
great poet to relieve the sternness of the father,
makes him also elevate the weakness of the son.
Jacopo hath no cowardice, save in leaving Venice.  Torture appals him not; he smiles at
death.  And how tragic *is* the death!

*Enter an Officer and Guards.*

Signor! the boat is at the shore—the wind
Is rising—we are ready to attend you.

### JACOPO FOSCARI.

And I to be attended.  Once more, father,
Your hand!

### DOGE.

Take it.  Alas! how thine own trembles!

### JACOPO FOSCARI.

No—you mistake; 'tis yours that shakes, my father.
Farewell!

### DOGE.

Is there aught else?

### JACOPO FOSCARI.

No—nothing.
Lend me your arm, good signor.  (*To the officer.*)

### OFFICER.

You turn pale,
Let me support you—paler—ho! some aid there!
Some water!

MARINA.

Ah, he is dying!

JACOPO FOSCARI.

Now, I'm ready—
My eyes swim strangely—where's the door?

MARINA.

Away!
Let *me* support him—my best love! Oh, God!
How faintly beats this heart—this pulse!

JACOPO FOSCARI.

The light
*Is* it the light?—I am faint.

[*Officer presents him with water.*

OFFICER.

He will be better,
Perhaps, in the air.

JACOPO FOSCARI.

I doubt not. Father—wife—
Your hands!

MARINA.

There's death in that damp clammy clasp.
Oh, God!—My Foscari, how fare you?

JACOPO FOSCARI.

Well! [*He dies.*

He dies; but where? In Venice—in the
light of that beloved sky—in the air of that de-
licious climate! He dies; but when? At the
moment he is about to leave that climate, that
sky, for ever! He might have said with another and a less glorious patriot of a later age,
" Il mio cadavere almeno non cadrà fra braccia

straniere ;......e le mie ossa poseranno su la
terra de' miei padri." Mark now, how the
pathos augments by the agency of the bereft
survivors.

OFFICER.

He's gone!

DOGE.

*He's free.*

MARINA.

No—no, he is not dead ;
There must be life yet in that heart—he could not
Thus leave me.

DOGE.

Daughter!

MARINA.

Hold thy peace, old man!
I am no daughter now—thou hast no son.
Oh, Foscari!

\* \* \* \* \*
\* \* \* \* \*

And how dreadly the whole force of the catastrophe is summed up, a few lines afterwards,
when, amidst the wailings of the widowed mother, the old Doge breaks forth—

My unhappy children!

MARINA.

What!
*You* feel it then at last—*you!*—Where is now
The Stoic of the State?

How you thrill at the savage yet natural taunt!
—how visibly you see the start of the wife!—

how audibly you hear the wild laugh and the
bitter words—

What!

——————————————— Where is now
The Stoic of the State ?

And how entirely the character of the Doge is
revealed ; how utter and dread becomes the anguish of the scene in the next *one* word :

DOGE (*throwing himself down by the body*).

HERE !

And at that word I doubt if the tragedy should
not have been concluded.   The vengeance of
Loredano—the completion of which makes the
catastrophe—is not so grand a termination as
the broken heart of the patriot exile, and the
broken pride of the patriot judge.

The same high notions of art which characterize these great dramas, are equally evinced
in the *Cain* and the *Sardanapalus :* the first,
which has more of the early stamp of Byron's
mind, is, for that reason perhaps, so well known,
and its merit so universally allowed, that I shall
not delay the reader by praising the Hercules
none have blamed.   One word only on the
*Sardanapalus.*

The genius developed in this tragedy is more
gorgeous and varied than in any other of By-

ron's works: the magnificent effeminacy, the unsettled courage, the regal generosity of Sardanapalus; the bold and hardy fervour of Arbaces the soldier, and the hoary craft of Beleses the priest, exhibit more extensive knowledge, and afford more glowing contrasts, than even the classic stateliness of Marino Faliero, or the deep pathos of the Foscari: And this drama, above all the rest of Byron's plays, is fitted for representation on the stage : the pomp of scene, the vitality and action of the plot, would, I am confident, secure it success among the multitude, who are more attracted by the external than the latent and less vivid sources of interest. But the chief beauty of this play is in the conception of Myrrha's character. This Greek girl, at once brave and tender, enamoured of her lord, yet yearning to be free; worshipping alike her distant land and the soft barbarian :—what new, and what dramatic combinations of feeling ! It is in this *struggle* of emotions, as I have said before, that the master-hand paints with the happiest triumph.

" Why," says Myrrha, reasoning with herself—

Why do I love this man ?   My country's daughters
Love none but heroes.   *But I have no country !*
The slave hath lost all save her bonds.   I love him;

And that's the heaviest link of the long chain—
To love whom we esteem not.      *      *

   *  *  *  *  *

He loves me, and I love him; the slave loves
Her master, and would free him from his vices.
If not, I have a means of freedom still,
And if I cannot teach him how to reign,
May show him how alone a king can leave
His throne.

The heroism of this fair Ionian is never above
nature, yet always on its highest verge. The
proud melancholy that mingles with her character, recalling her father-land—her warm and generous love, "without self-love"—her passionate
and Greek desire to elevate the nature of Sardanapalus, that she may the better justify her
own devotion—the grave and yet sweet sternness that pervades her gentler qualities, exhi-
biting itself in fidelity without fear, and enabling
her to hold with a steady hand the torch that
shall consume on the pyre (made sacred to her
religion by the memory of its own Alcides) both
the Assyrian and the Greek; all these combinations are the result of the purest sentiment
and the noblest art. Her last words at the
pyre sustain the great conception of her character. With the natural yearning of the Achaian,
her thoughts in that moment revert to her distant clime, recalled, however, at once to her

perishing lord beside her, and uniting, almost
in one breath, the two contending affections.

> Farewell, thou earth!
> And loveliest spot of earth! farewell, Ionia!
> Be thou still free and beautiful, and far
> Aloof from desolation!  My last prayer
> Was for thee, my last thoughts, save *one*, were of thee!

SARDANAPALUS.

And that?

MYRRHA.

*Is yours.*

The plot of the drama is worthy the creation of its heroine.  The fall of a mighty Em-
pire; the vivid incarnation of a dark and remote
time; the primeval craft of the priest conspiring
with the rough ambition of the soldier, (main
origin of great changes in the world's earlier
years;) the splendid and august catastrophe;
the most magnificent suicide the earth ever
knew!—what a field for genius! what a conception worthy of its toils!

Nothing has been more constantly asserted of
Byron than his want of variety in character.
Every criticism tells us that he never paints but
one person, in whatever costume; that the dress
may vary, but the lay figure remains the same.
Never was any popular fallacy more absurd!
It is true that the dogma holds good with the

early poems, but is entirely contradicted in the later plays. Where, in the whole range of fiction, are there any characters more strongly contrasted, more essentially various and dissimilar, than Sardanapalus, the Assyrian king, and Marino Faliero, the Venetian Doge;—than Beleses, the rugged priest, cut out of the marble of nature; and Jacopo Foscari, moulded from the kindliest of the southern elements;—than the passionate Marina, the delicate and queenly Angiolina, the heroic Myrrha—the beautiful incarnation of her own mythology? To name these is sufficient to refute an assertion hitherto so credulously believed, and which may serve as an illustration of the philosophy of popular criticism. From the first works of an author the standard is drawn by which he is compared; and in no instance are the sins of the parents more unfortunately visited on the children.

Yet why, since the tragedies evince so matured and profound a genius, are they so incalculably less popular than the early poems? It may be said, that the dramatic form itself is an obstacle to popularity; yet scarcely so, for I am just old enough distinctly to remember the intense and universal curiosity with which the public awaited the appearance of *The Doge of*

*Venice;* the eagerness with which it was read, and the disappointment which it occasioned. Had the dramatic form been the cause of its unpopularity, it would have occasioned for it at the first a cool and lukewarm reception: the welcome which greeted its announcement is a proof that the disappointment was occasioned by the materials of the play, and not *because* it was a play. Besides, *Manfred,* one of the most admired of all Byron's works, was cast in the dramatic mould. One cause of the comparative unpopularity of the plays is, perhaps, that the *style* is less rich and musical than that of the poems; but the principal cause is *in that very versatility, that very coming out from self, the want of which has been so superficially complained of.* The characters were beautifully conceived; but they represented not that character which we expected, and yearned to see. That mystic and idealized shape, in which we beheld ourselves, had receded from the scene —we missed that touching egotism which was the expression of the Universal Heart—across the enchanted mirror new shadows passed, but it was our own likeness that we desired— the likeness of those deep and cherished feelings with which the poet had identified himself! True, that he still held the glass to human nature; but it was no longer to that aspect of nature which we most coveted to behold, and to which custom had not yet brought satiety. This was the true cause of our disappointment. Byron now addressed the passion, and the sentiment, and the thought, common to *all* time, but no longer those peculiar to the temper of the age—

> Our friend was to the dead,
> *To us he died when first he parted from us.*
>
> \* \* \* \* \*
>
> He stood beside us, like our youth,
> Transform'd for us the real to a dream,
> Clothing the palpable and the familiar
> With golden exhalations of the dawn.†

The disappointment we experienced when Byron departed from the one ideal image, in which alone our egotism loved to view him, is made yet more visible in examining his character than in analyzing his works. We grow indignant against him in proportion, not as we find him unworthy as a man, but departing from the attributes in which our imagination had clothed him. He was to the Public as a lover to his mistress, who forgives a crime more easily than a foible, and in whom the judgment becomes acute only in proportion as the imagination is undeceived. Had the lives, the sketches, the details, which

† Coleridge's *Wallenstein.*

have appeared subsequently to his early and poetical death, but sustained our own illusions—
had they preserved " the shadow and the majesty" with which we had enveloped his image,
they might have represented him as far more erring than he appears to have been, and we should
have forgiven whatever crimes were consistent
with the dark but lofty nature we ascribed to
him. But weakness, insincerity, the petty caprice, the womanish passion, the vulgar pride,
or even the coarse habit—these we forgave not,
for they shocked and mocked our own self-love;
they were as sardonic reproaches on the blind
fallacy of our own judgment; they lowered the
ideal in our own breasts; they humbled the
vanity of our own nature; we had associated
the poet with ourselves; we had felt *his* emotions
as the refining, the exalted expression of *ours*,
and whatever debased our likeness, debased
ourselves! through his foibles our self-love was
wounded: he was the great Representative of
the Poetry of our own hearts; and, wherever he
seemed unfaithful to his trust, we resented it as
a treason to the majesty of our common cause.

But perhaps the hour in which we most
deeply felt how entirely we had wound and
wrapt our own poetry in himself, was that in
which the news of his death reached this coun-

try.  Never shall I forget the singular, the stunning sensation, which the intelligence produced.  I was exactly at that age, half man and half boy, in which the poetical sympathies are most keen—among the youth of that day a growing diversion from Byron to Shelley and Wordsworth had just commenced—but the moment in which we heard he was no more, united him to us at once, without a rival.  We could not believe that the bright race was run.  So much of us died with him, that the notion of his death had something of the unnatural, of the impossible.  It was as if a part of the mechanism of the very world stood still:—that we had ever questioned—that we had ever blamed him, was a thought of absolute remorse, and all our ,worship of his genius was not half so strongly felt as our love for himself.

When he went down to dust, it was as the abrupt close of some history of deep passion in our actual lives,—the interest—the excitement of years came to a gloomy pause—

> His last sigh
> Dissolved the charm—the disenchanted earth
> Lost all her lustre—Where her glittering towers,
> Her golden mountains, where? all darken'd down
> To naked waste—a dreary vale of years!
> THE GREAT MAGICIAN'S DEAD!*

---

* Young.

Exaggerated as this language may seem to our children, our contemporaries know that all words are feeble to express the universal feeling of England at that lonely death-bed in a foreign land, amidst wild and savage strangers, far from the sister, the wife, the child, whose names faltered on the lips of the dying man,—closing in desolation a career of sadness—rendering his latest sigh to the immemorial land which had received his earliest song, and where henceforth and for ever

Shall Death and Glory a joint sabbath keep.

Even now, at this distance of time, all the feelings that then rushed upon us, melt upon me once more. Dissenting as I now do from much of the vague admiration his more popular works receive, and seeing in himself much that Virtue must lament, and even Wisdom contemn, I cannot but think of him as of some early friend, associating with himself all the brightest reminiscences of youth, burying in his grave a poetry of existence that can never be restored, and of whom every harsh sentence, even while not unfaithful to truth, is dishonouring to the fidelity of love—

"The Beautiful is vanished and returns not."

I have dwelt thus much upon Byron, partly because though the theme is hacknied, it is not exhausted*—partly because I perceive an unjust and indiscriminate spirit of depreciation springing up against that great poet (and I hold it the duty of a critic to oppose zealously the caprice and change of mere fashions in opinion)—and principally, because, in reviewing the intellectual spirit of the age, it is necessary to point out at some length the manner in which its most celebrated representative illustrated and identified it with himself.

But while my main task is with the more popular influences of the intellectual spirit of the present day, I must not pass over in silence that deep under-current which in all ages is formed by some writers whose influence floats not on the surface. The sound of their lyres, not loud to the near listener, travels into distance, enduring, deep, and through prolonged vibrations, buoying itself along the immeasurable waves of space. From amidst writers of this class I single out but two, Wordsworth and Shelley. I believe that both these poets have been influential to a degree perfectly

* In advancing, too, the doctrine, which if not quite new, is at least unpopular, that his Dramas are better than his early poems, it was necessary to go somewhat into the conception of those Dramas.

unguessed by those who look only to their popularity ; and, above all, I believe that of Wordsworth, especially, to have been an influence of
a more noble and purely intellectual character
than any writer of our age and nation has exercised. Wordsworth's genius is peculiarly German. This assertion may startle those who
have been accustomed to believe the German
genius only evinced by extravagant tales, bom-
bastic passion, and mystical *diableries.* Wordsworth is German from his singular household-
ness of feeling — from the minute and accurate
manner with which he follows his ardour for
Nature into the smaller links and harmonies
which may be considered as her details. He
has not, it is true, " the many-sidedness" of
Göthe ; but he closely resembles a *certain* portion of Göthe's mind, viz. the reverential, contemplative, self-tasking disposition to the study
of all things appertaining to THE NATURAL :
his ideas, too, fall into that refined and refining *toryism,* the result of a mingled veneration for the past — of a disdain for the pettier
cries which float over that vast abyss which
we call the public, and of a firm desire for
Peace as the best nurse to high and undiurnal
thoughts, which so remarkably distinguishes
the great artist of Tasso and Wilhelm Meis-

ter. This toryism—(I so call it for want of a better name)—is one of which only very high minds are capable ; it is the product of a most deep if untrue philosophy : no common Past-worshippers can understand or share it, just as no vulgar sceptics can comprehend the ethereal scepticism of a Spinosa. That Wordsworth's peculiar dogmas should lead him into occasional, (nay, to my taste, frequent) error, is saying of him what we must say of every man of enthusiasm who adopts a system ; but, be it observed, it only misleads him in that part of his writings which arrogate " simplicity," and in which, studying to be simple, he becomes often artificial ; it never misleads him in his advances to " sublimity :" here he is always natural ; he rises without effort, and the circumfusing holiness of his mind bathes with a certain religious grandeur the commonest words and the most familiar thoughts. But what temper of the times does Wordsworth represent, and in what is he a teacher ? Let us reflect. Whenever there is a fierce contest between opposing parties, it usually happens that to each party there is a small and scarce-calculated band inspired and led by far more spiritualized and refining thoughts than the rest, who share not the passion, nor the feud, nor the human and coarser motives which actuate the noisier herd. Of one of these parties Wordsworth is the representative; of the other, Shelley. Wordsworth is the apostle, the spiritualizer of those who cling to the most idealized part of things that are—Religion and her houses, Loyalty and her monuments—the tokens of the Sanctity which overshadows the Past: these are of him, and he of them. Shelley, on the other hand, in his more impetuous, but equally intellectual and unworldly mind, is the spiritualizer of all who forsake the past and the present, and with lofty hopes and a bold philanthropy, rush forward into the future, attaching themselves not only to things unborn, but to speculations founded on unborn things. Both are representatives of a class of thought, refined, remote, belonging to the age, but not to the louder wranglers of the age. Scott and Byron are poets representing a philosophy resulting from the passions, or, at least, the action, of life; Shelley and Wordsworth represent that which arises from the intellect, and belongs to the Contemplative or the Ideal. It is natural that the first two should have a large audience, and the two latter a select one; for so far have they (the last) gone into the remoter and more abstract ideas, and wrought poetry from science, that they may be said to appeal to us less as poets than as metaphysicians, and have therefore obtained the homage and the circle which belong to the reasoner rather than the wider worship of the bard ; but each appertains emphatically to a time of visible and violent transition — the one preserving all the beauty of the time past, the other with a more youthful genius bodying forth the beauty of a time to be. Each is an equal servitor to knowledge, if we may trust to the truth of Wordsworth's simile, the sublimest in recent poetry—

> " Past and Future are the wings
> On whose support harmoniously conjoin'd,
> Moves the great Spirit of Human Knowledge."

But I think, of the two, that Wordsworth has exercised on the present day the more beneficial influence ; for if, as I have held, and shall again have occasion to repeat,

> " The world is too much with us,"

if the vice of the time leans to the Material, and produces a low-born taste and an appetite for coarse excitement,—Wordsworth's poetry is of all existing in the world the most calculated to refine—to etherealize—to exalt ;—to offer the most correspondent counterpoise to the scale that inclines to earth. It is for this that I consider his influence mainly beneficial. His poetry has repaired to us the want of an immaterial philosophy—nay it *is* philosophy, and it is of the immaterial school. No writer more unvulgarizes the mind. His circle is small—but for that very reason the votaries are more attached. They preserve in the working-day world the holy sabbath of his muse — and doubtless they will perpetuate that tranquillising worship from generation to generation, till the devotion of the few shall grow into the custom of the many.

Shelley, with a more daring and dramatic* genius, with greater mastery of language, and the true Lucretian soul, for ever aspiring *extra flammantia mœnia mundi*, is equally intellectual in his creations; and despite the young audacity which led him into denying a God,

---

* Had Shelley lived, I understand from his friends that he would probably have devoted himself especially to the drama. The Cençi is the only one of his writings which contains human interest—and if Shelley's metaphysical flights had been once tamed down to the actual flesh and blood characters which the drama exacts, there is little doubt but that as his judgment improved in the choice of subject and the conception of plot, he would have been our greatest dramatist since Shakspeare. But

" Gemuit sub pondere cymba."

his poetry is of a remarkably ethereal and spi-
ritualizing cast. It is steeped in veneration—it
is for ever thirsting for the Heavenly and the
Immortal—and the Deity he questioned avenges
Himself only by impressing His image upon all
that the poet undertook. But Shelley at present has subjected himself to be misunderstood ;
he has become the apologist for would-be mys-
tics, and dreamers of foolish dreams,—for an
excellent master may obtain worthless disciples,
just as the young voluptuaries of the Garden
imagined vice was sanctioned by Epicurus, and
the juvenile casuists of schools have learned
Pyrrhonism from Berkeley. The blinding glitter of his diction, the confusion produced on an
unsteady mind by the rapid whirl of his daz-
zling thoughts, have assisted in the formation
of a false school of poetry,—a school of sound-
ing words and unintelligible metaphysics — a
school of crude and bewildered jargonists, who
talk of "the everlasting heart of things," and
the "genius of the world," and such phrases,
which are the terms of a system with Shelley,
and are merely fine expressions with his followers. An imitator of Wordsworth must come at
once to Nature : he may be puerile, he may be
prosaic—but he cannot go far from the Natural.
The yearning of Wordsworth's genius is like

the patriotism of certain travellers, who in their remotest wanderings carry with them a portion of their native earth. But Shelley's less settled and more presuming faculty deals little with the Seen and Known — it is ever with the spectral images of things, chasing the invisible Echo, and grasping at the bodiless Shadow. Whether he gives language to Pan, to Asia, to Demiurgus, or song to the Cloud, or paints the river love of Alpheus for Arethusa, or follows, through all the gorgeous windings of his most wondrous diction, the spirit of Poesy in Alastor, or that of Liberty in the Revolt of Islaam—he is tasking our interest for things that are not mundane or familiar—things which he alone had power to bind to Nature, and which those who imitate him leave utterly dissevered from her control. They, too, deal with demigods and phantoms—the beautiful Invisibles of creation; but they forget the chain by which the Jupiter of their creed linked each, the highest to the lowest, in one indissoluble connexion, that united even the highest heaven to the bosom of our common earth.

I think, then, that so far as this age is considered, (although for posterity, when true worshippers are substituted for false disciples, it may be otherwise,) Shelley's influence, both poetical

and moral, has been far less purifying and salutary than Wordsworth's. But both are men of
a purer, perhaps a higher, intellectual order than
either Byron or Scott, and although not possessing the same mastery over the more daily
emotions, and far more limited in their range of
power than their rival " Kings of Verse," they
have yet been the rulers of more unworldly
subjects, and the founders of a more profound
and high-wrought dynasty of opinion.

It seems, then, that in each of these four
great poets the Imaginative Literature has arrogated the due place of the Philosophical.

In the several characters of their genius,
embodying the truth of the times, will the
moral investigator search for the expression of
those thoughts which make the aspect of an
era, and, while they reflect the present age,
prepare the next. It is thus that, from time
to time, the Imagination assumes the natural
office of the Reason, and is the parent of Revolutions, because the organ of Opinion: And to
this, the loftiest, moral effect of imaginative literature, many of its superficial decriers have been
blind. " The mind," saith the Stagyrite, " has
over the body the control which a master exercises over his slave: but the Reason has over
the Imagination that control which a magistrate

possesses over a freeman"—" who," adds Bacon
in his noble comment on the passage, " *may
come to rule in his turn*." At the same time that
Lycurgus reformed Sparta, he introduced into
Greece the poems of Homer ;—which act was
the more productive of heroes ?—which wrought
the more important results upon the standard of
legislative morals, or exercised the more permanent influence upon the destiny of states?

I return to the more wide, and popular, and
important impression, made upon the times.
Göthe has told us, that when he had written
*Werther,* he felt like a sinner relieved from the
burden of his errors by a general confession ; and
he became, as it were, inspired with energy to
enter on a new existence. The mind of a great
writer is the type of the general mind. The
public, at certain periods, oppressed with a peculiar weight of passion, or of thought, require
to throw it off by expression ; once expressed,
they rarely return to it again : they pass into a
fresh intellectual gradation; they enter with
Göthe into a new existence ; hence one reason
of the ill-success of imitators—they repeat a
tone we no longer have a desire to hear. When
Byron passed away, the feeling he had represented craved utterance no more. With a sigh
we turned to the actual and practical career

of life : we awoke from the morbid, the passionate, the dreaming, " the moonlight and the dimness of the mind," and by a natural reaction
addressed ourselves to the active and daily objects which lay before us. And this with the
more intenseness, because the death of a great
poet invariably produces an indifference to the
art itself. We can neither bear to see him imitated, nor yet contrasted ; we preserve the impression, but we break the mould. Hence that
strong attachment to the Practical, which became so visible a little time after the death of
Byron, and which continues (unabated, or rather
increased,) to characterize the temper of the
time. Insensibly acted upon by the doctrine
of the Utilitarians, we desired to see Utility in
every branch of intellectual labour. Byron, in
his severe comments upon England, and his
satire on our social system, had done much
that has not yet been observed, in shaking off
from the popular mind certain of its strongest
national prejudices ; and the long Peace, and
the pressure of financial difficulties, naturally
inclined us to look narrowly at our real state ;
to examine the laws we had only boasted of, and
dissect the constitution we had hitherto deemed
it only our duty to admire. We were in the
situation of a man who, having run a certain

career of dreams and extravagance, begins to be prudent and saving, to calculate his conduct, and to look to his estate. Politics thus gradually and commonly absorbed our attention, and we grew to identify ourselves, our feelings, and our cause, with statesmen and economists instead of with poets and refiners. Thus, first Canning, and then Brougham, may be said, for a certain time, to have represented, more than any other individuals, the common Intellectual Spirit; and the interest usually devoted to the imaginative, was transferred to the real.

In the mean while, the more than natural distaste for poetry that succeeded the death of Byron had increased the appetite for prose fictions; the excitement of the fancy, pampered by the melo-dramatic tales which had become the rage in verse, required food even when verse grew out of fashion. The new career that Walter Scott had commenced tended also somewhat to elevate with the vulgar a class of composition that, with the educated, required no factitious elevation; for, with the latter, what new dignity could be thrown upon a branch of letters that Cervantes, Fielding, Le Sage, Voltaire, and Fenelon had already made only less than Epic? It was not, however, as in former times, the great novel alone, that was read among the more refined circles, but novels of all sorts. Unlike poetry, the name itself was an attraction. In these works, even to the lightest and most ephemeral, something of the moral spirit of the age betrayed itself. The novels of fashionable life illustrate feelings very deeply rooted, and productive of no common revolution. In proportion as the aristocracy had become social, and fashion allowed the members of the more mediocre classes a hope to outstep the boundaries of fortune, and be quasi-aristocrats themselves, people eagerly sought for representations of the manners which they aspired to imitate, and the circles to which it was not impossible to belong. But as with emulation discontent also was mixed, as many hoped to be called and few found themselves chosen, so a satire on the follies and vices of the great gave additional piquancy to the description of their lives. There was a sort of social fagging established; the fag loathed his master, but not the system by which one day or other he himself might be permitted to fag. What the world would not have dared to gaze upon, had it been gravely exhibited by a philosopher, (so revolting a picture of the aristocracy would it have seemed,) they praised with avidity in the light sketches of a novelist. Hence the three-years' run of the fashionable novels was a shrewd sign of the times; straws they were, but they showed the upgathering of the storm. Those novels were the most successful which hit off one or the other of the popular cravings —the desire to dissect fashion, or the wish to convey utility—those which affected to combine both, as the novels of Mr. Ward, were the most successful of all.

Few writers ever produced so great an effect on the political spirit of their generation as some of these novelists, who, without any other merit, unconsciously exposed the falsehood, the hypocrisy, the arrogant and vulgar insolence of patrician life. Read by all classes, in every town, in every village, these works, as I have before stated, could not but engender a mingled indignation and disgust at the parade of frivolity, the ridiculous disdain of truth, nature, and mankind, the self-consequence and absurdity, which, falsely or truly, these novels exhibited as a picture of aristocratic society. The Utilitarians railed against them, and they were effecting with unspeakable rapidity the very purposes the Utilitarians desired.

While these light works were converting the multitude, graver writers were soberly confirming their effect, society itself knew not the change in feeling which had crept

over it; till a sudden flash, as it were, revealed the change electrically to itself. Just
at the time when with George the Fourth an
*old* era expired, the excitement of a popular
election at home concurred with the three days
of July in France, to give a decisive tone
to the *new*. The question of Reform came on,
and to the astonishment of the nation itself,
it was hailed at once by the national heart.
From that moment, the intellectual spirit
hitherto partially directed to, became *wholly*
absorbed in, politics; and whatever lighter
works have since obtained a warm and general
hearing, have either developed the errors of the
social system, or the vices of the legislative.
Of the first, I refrain from giving an example ;
of the last, I instance as a sign of the times,
the searching fictions of Miss Martineau, and
the wide reputation they have acquired.

A description of the mere frivolities of fashion
is no longer coveted ; for the public mind, once
settled towards an examination of the aristocracy, has pierced from the surface to the depth ;
it has *probed* the wound, and it now desires to
*cure*.

It is in this state that the Intellectual Spirit
of the age rests, demanding the Useful, but pre-

pared to receive it through familiar shapes:
a state at present favourable to ordinary knowledge, to narrow views, or to mediocre genius;
but adapted to prepare the way and to found
success for the coming triumphs of a bold philosophy, or a profound and subtile imagination.  Some cause, indeed, there is of fear, lest
the desire for immediate and palpable utility
should stint the capacities of genius to the trite
and familiar truths.  But as Criticism takes a
more wide and liberal view of the true and
unbounded sphere of the Beneficial, we may
trust that this cause of fear will be removed.
The passions of men are the most useful field
for the metaphysics of the imagination, and yet
the grandest and the most inexhaustible.  Let
us take care that we do not, as in the old Greek
fable, cut the wings of our bees and set flowers
before them, as the most sensible mode of filling
the Hives of Truth !

But the great prevailing characteristic of the
present intellectual spirit is one most encouraging to human hopes; it is Benevolence.  There
has grown up among us a sympathy with the
great mass of mankind.  For this we are indebted in no small measure to the philosophers
(with whom Benevolence is, in all times, the

foundation of philosophy); and that more decided and emphatic expression of the sentiment
which was common, despite of their errors, to
the French moralists of the last century, has been
kept alive and applied to immediate legislation
by the English moralists of the present. We owe
also the popularity of the growing principle to
the writings of Miss Edgeworth and of Scott,
who sought their characters among the peolpe,
and who interested us by a picture of (and not a
declamation upon) their life and its humble vicis-
situdes, their errors and their virtues. We owe
it also, though unconsciously, to the gloomy
misanthropy of Byron; for proportioned to the
intenseness with which we shared that feeling
was the reaction from which we awoke from it ;
and amongst the more select and poetical of
us, we owe it yet more to the dreaming philanthropy of Shelley, and the patriarchal tenderness of Wordsworth. It is this feeling that
we should unite to sustain and to develope. It
has come to us pure and bright from the ordeal
of years—the result of a thousand errors—but
born, if we preserve it, as their healer and
redemption.

Diodorus Siculus tells us, that the forest of
the Pyrenean mountains being set on fire, and
the heat penetrating to the soil, a pure stream

of silver gushed forth from the earth's bosom, and revealed for the first time the existence of those mines afterwards so celebrated.

It is thus from causes apparently the most remote, and often amidst the fires that convey to us, at their first outbreaking, images only of terror and desolation, that we deduce the most precious effects, and discover the treasures to enrich the generations that are to come !

# CHAPTER III.

I THINK, sir, that when our ingenious coun-
tryman, Joshua Barnes, gave us so notable an
account of the Pigmies, he must, in the spirit of
prophecy, have intended to allegorize the em-
pire of the Penny Periodicals.  For, in the
first place, these little strangers seem, Pigmy-
like, of a marvellous ferocity and valour; they
make great head against their foes—they spread
themselves incontinently—they possess the land
—they live but a short time, yet are plenteously
prolific; they owe much to what the learned
Joshua terms " the royal Lescha," viz. a certain society (evidently the foretype of that lately
established under the patronage of my Lord
Brougham)—set up as he sheweth " for the increase and propagation of experimental know-

ledge;" above all, and a most blissful pecu-
liarity it is, *"for taxes, they are wholly unacquainted with them!"* they make vigilant war
against the cranes, who I take it are pal-
pably designed for tax-gatherers in general,
*quocunque gaudentes nomine*—a fact rendered
clear to the plainest understanding by the following description of these predatory birds :

" The cranes being the only causers of fa-
mine in the land, by reason they are so numerous that they can devour the most plentiful
harvest, both by eating the seeds beforehand,
and then picking the ears that remain."

Certes, however, these little gentry seem of
a more general ambition than their Pigmæan
types ; for the latter confined themselves to a
limited territory " from Gadazalia to Elysiana ;"
but these, the pigmies of our time, overrun us
altogether, and push, with the rude insolence of
innovation, our most venerable folios from their
stools. The rage for cheap publications is not
limited to Penny Periodicals; family libraries of
all sorts have been instituted, with the capti-
vating profession of teaching all things useful
—bound in cloth, for the sum of five shillings
a month ! Excellent inventions, which, after
showing us the illimitable ingenuity of compilation, have at length fallen the prey of their

own numbers, and buried themselves amongst the corpses of the native quartos which they so successfully invaded.

Cheap publications are excellent things in themselves. Whatever increases the reading public, tends necessarily to equalize the knowledge already in the world ; but the process by which knowledge is equalized is not altogether that by which the degree of knowledge is heightened. Cheap publications of themselves are sufficient for the *diffusion* of knowledge, but not for its *advancement*. The schoolmaster equalizes information, by giving that which he possesses to others, and for that very reason can devote but little time to increasing his own stock.

Let me make this more familiar by telling you an anecdote of our friend Dr. ——. You know that he is a man of the very highest scientific attainments ? You know also that he is not overburdened with those same precious metals on the history of which he can so learnedly descant. He took a book some months ago to a publisher of enterprise and capital : it was full of the profoundest research ; the bookseller shook his head, and—

" Pray, sir," said he, musingly, " how many persons in England are acquainted with the ultimate principles by which you come to your result ?"

" Not fifty, sir," cried the doctor, with all the enthusiasm of a discoverer.

" And how many can understand the elementary principles which occupy your first chapter ?"

" Oh !" said the doctor, with indifference, " *those* principles are merely plain truths in mechanics, which most manufacturers ought to know, and which many literary dandies think it shows learning to allude to ; perhaps, therefore, several thousands may be familiar with the contents of the first chapter ; but, I assure you, sir, you don't get far before"—

" Pardon me, doctor," interrupted the bookseller, shortly—" if you address the fifty persons, you must publish this work on your own account ; if you address the thousands, why it is quite another matter. Here is your MS. ; burn all but the first chapter : as a commercial speculation, the rest is mere rubbish ; if you will then spin out the first chapter into a volume, and call it *The Elements of* —— *Familiarly Explained*—why, I think, sir, with your name, I could afford you three hundred pounds for it."

Necessity knows no law. *The Elements* are

published to teach new thousands what other
thousands knew before, and the *Discoveries* lie
in the doctor's desk, where they will only become lucrative, when some richer man shall
invent and propagate them, and the public
will call on the poor doctor " to make them
familiar."

Now observe a very curious consequence
from this story: Suppose a certain science is
*only* cultivated by five hundred men, and that
they have all cultivated the science to a certain
height. A book that should tell them what
they knew already, they would naturally not
purchase, and a book that told them more than
they knew they would eagerly buy ; in such a
case, the doctor's position would have been re-
versed, and his *Discoveries* would have been
much more lucrative to him than his *Elements*.
—Thus we may observe, that the tone of knowledge is usually more scholastic in proportion as
the circle of readers is confined.   When scholars
are your audience, you address them after the
fashion of a scholar.   Hence, formerly, every
man thought it necessary, when he wrote a
book, to bestow upon its composition the most
scrupulous care; to fill its pages with the product of a studious life; to polish its style with
the classic file, and to ornament its periods with

the academical allusion. He knew that the majority of those who read his work would be able to appreciate labour or to detect neglect; but, as the circle of readers increased, the mind of the writer became less fastidious; the superficial readers had outnumbered the profounder critics. He still addressed the majority, but the taste of the majority was no longer so scrupulous as to the fashion of the address. Since the Revival of Letters itself, the more confined the public, the more laborious the student. Ascham is more scholastic than Raleigh; Raleigh than Addison; and Addison than Scott.

The spirit of a popular assembly can enter into the crowd you write for, as well as the crowd you address; and a familiar frankness, or a superficial eloquence, charms the assembly when full, which a measured wisdom and a copious knowledge were necessary to win, when its numbers were scattered and select.

It is natural that writers should be ambitious of creating a sensation: a sensation is produced by gaining the ear, not of the few, but the many; it is natural, therefore, that they should address the many; the style pleasing to the many becomes, of course, the style most frequently aimed at: hence the profusion of amusing, familiar, and superficial writings. People complain of it, as if it were a proof of degeneracy in the knowledge of authors—it is a proof of the increased number of readers. The time is come when nobody will fit out a ship for the intellectual Columbus to discover new worlds, but when everybody will subscribe for his setting up a steam-boat between Calais and Dover. You observe then, sir, (consequences which the fine talkers of the day have wholly overlooked) that the immense superficies of the public operates two ways in deteriorating from the profundity of writers : in the first place, it renders it no longer necessary for an author to make himself profound before he writes ; and in the next place, it encourages those authors who *are* profound, by every inducement, not of lucre alone, but of fame, to exchange deep writing for agreeable writing : the voice which animates the man ambitious of wide fame, does not, according to the beautiful line in Rogers, whisper to him " ASPIRE," but " DESCEND." " He stoops to conquer." Thus, if we look abroad, in France, where the reading public is less numerous than in England,* a more elevated and refining tone is more fashionable in literature ; and in America, where it is infinitely larger, the

* In France, the proportion of those educated in schools is but one in twenty-eight.

tone of literature is infinitely more superficial. It is possible, that the high-souled among literary men, desirous rather of truth than fame, or willing to traverse their trial to posterity, are actuated, *unconsciously*, by the spirit of the times; but actuated they necessarily are, just (to return to my former comparison) as the wisest orator, who uttered only philosophy to a thin audience of sages, mechanically abandons his refinements and his reasonings, and expands into a louder tone and more familiar manner as the assembly increases;—the temper of the popular meeting is unavoidably caught by the mind that addresses it.

From these remarks we may perceive then, that in order to increase the height of knowledge, it is not sufficient to diffuse its extent; nay, that in that very diffusion there is a tendency to the superficial, which requires to be

* M. Cousin, speaking of professors who in despair of a serious audience, wish at least for a numerous one, has well illustrated this principle. "Dans ce cas c'en est fait de la science, car on a beau faire, on se proportionne à son auditoire. Il y a dans les grandes foules je ne sais quel ascendant presque magnétique, qui subjugue les ames les plus fermes; et tel qui eût été un professeur sérieux et instructif pour une centaine d'étudiens attentifs, devient leger et superficiel avec un auditoire superficiel et leger."

VOL. II.

counteracted.  And this, sir, it seems to me
that we can only thoroughly effect by the Endowments of which I have before spoken.  For
since the government of knowledge is like that
of states, and instituted not for the power of
the few, but the enjoyment of the many, so
this *diffusion* of information amongst the ignorant is greatly to be commended and encouraged, even though it operate unfavourably
on the *increase* of information amongst the
learned.  We ought not, therefore, to resist,
even were we able, which we are not, the
circulation of intelligence ; but by other means
we should seek to supply the reservoirs, from
which, aloft and remote, the fertilizing waters
are supplied.  I see not that this can be
done by any other means than the establishment of such professorships, and salaries for the
cultivators of the highest branches of literature
and science, as may be adequate, both in the
number and in the income allotted to each, to
excite ambition.  Thus a tribunal for high
endeavour will be established, independent of
the court of the larger public, independent
indeed, yet each acting upon the other.  The
main difficulty would be that of appointing fit
electors to these offices.  I cannot help thinking that there should, for the sake of emulation,

and the prevention of corruption or prejudice, be different electoral bodies, that should promote to vacancies in rotation ; and these might be the three branches of the legislature, the different national universities, and, above all, (though the notion may seem extravagant at first sight,) foreign academies, which being wholly free from sectarian, or party prejudices, would, I am convinced, nine times out of ten, (until at least they had aroused our emulation by exciting our shame,) choose the most fitting persons : For foreign nations are to the higher efforts of genius, the Representatives of Posterity itself. This, to be sure, is not a scheme ever likely to be realised ; neither, I confess, is it wholly free from objections : but unless some such incitement to the loftier branches of knowledge be devised, the increasing demand will only introduce adulteration in the supply. So wide a popularity, and so alluring a remuneration, being given to the superficial, whoever is ambitious, and whoever is poor, will naturally either suit his commodity to the market, or renounce his calling altogether. At present, a popular instructor is very much like a certain master in Italian, who has thriven prodigiously upon a new experiment on his pupils. J—— was a clever fellow, and full of knowledge which nobody wanted to know. After seeing him in rags for some years, I met him the other day most sprucely attired, and with the complacent and sanguine air of a prosperous gentleman :—

" I am glad to see, my dear sir," said I, " that the world wags well with you."

" It does."

" Doubtless, your books sell famously."

" Bah ! no bookseller will buy them : no, sir, I have hit on a better *metier* than that of writing books—I am giving lessons in Italian."

" Italian ! why I thought when I last saw you, that you told me Italian was the very language you knew nothing about ?"

" Nor did I, sir ; but directly I had procured scholars, I began to teach myself. I bought a dictionary ; I learnt that lesson in the morning which I taught my pupils at noon. I found I was more familiar and explanatory, thus *fresh from knowing little*, than if I had been confused and over deep by knowing much. I am a most popular teacher, sir ;—and my whole art consists in being just one lesson in advance of my scholars !"

# CHAPTER IV.

## STYLE.

More clear, natural and warm than formerly — but less erudite, and polished—More warm, but more liable to extravagance—Cause of the success of fiction—Mr. Starch and his dogmas—Every great writer corrupts his language—The Classic School and the Romantic—*Our* writers have united the two.

IF the observations in my last chapter be correct, and books become less learned in proportion as the reading community becomes more numerous, it is evident that in the same proportion, and for the same cause, style will become less elaborate and polished than when the author, addressing only the scholastic few, found a critic in every reader. Writings addressed to the multitude must be clear and concise: the style of the present day has therefore gained in clearness what it has lost in erudition.

A numerous audience require also, before all things, a natural and frank manner in him who addresses them; they have no toleration for the didascalic affectations in which academicians delight. " Speak out, and like a man !" is their first exclamation to one who seems about to be mincing and pedantic in his accost, or set and prepared in the fashion of his periods. Style, therefore, at the present day, is generally more plain and straightforward than heretofore, and tells its unvarnished tale with little respect to the balanced cadence and the elaborate sentence. It has less of the harmony of the prepared, and more of the vigour of the extempore. At the same time it is to be regretted that the higher and more refining beauties should be neglected —the delicate allusion—the subtle grace. It would be well could we preserve *both* the simplicity and the richness—aiming at an eloquence like that of the Roman orator, which, while seeming to flow most freely, harmonized every accent to an accompanying music.

From the same cause which gives plainness to the modern style, it receives also warmth, and seems entirely to have escaped from the solemn frigidity of Johnson, and the silver fetters that clanked on the graceful movements of Goldsmith, or the measured elegance of Hume. But, on the other hand, this warmth frequently runs into extravagance, and as the orator to a crowd says that with vehemence which to a few

he would say with composure, so the main fault
of the present style, especially of the younger
writers, is often in an exaggerated tone and a
superfluous and gratuitous assumption of energy
and passion. It is this failing, carried with
them to a greater extent than it is with us,
which burlesques the romantic French writers
of the present day, and from which *we* are only
preserved by a more manly and sturdy audience.

As with the increase of the crowd, appeals to
passion become more successful, so in the en-
largement of the reading public I see one great
cause of the unprecedented success of fiction.
Some inconsiderate critics prophesy that the
taste for novels and romances will wear itself
out; it is, on the contrary, more likely to increase as the circle of the public widens. Fiction, with its graphic delineations and appeals to
the familiar emotions, is adapted to the crowd—
for it is the oratory of literature.

You are acquainted with Mr. Starch. He is
a man who professes a vast regard for what he
calls *the original purity of the language.* He is
bitterly opposed to new words. He hath made
two bugbears to his mind — the one hight
' Latinity,' the other ' Gallicism.' He seeth these
spectres in every modern composition. He
valueth himself upon writing Saxon, and his

style walketh about as naked as a Pict.  In
fact nothing can be more graceless and bald
than his compositions, and yet he calls *them*
only " the true English."   But he is very
much mistaken ; they are not such English as
any English writer, worth reading at least, ever
wrote.  At what period, sir, would the critics
of Starch's order stop the progress of our language ?  to what elements would they reduce it ?
The language is like the land,—restore it to
what it was for the aboriginals, and you would
reduce beauty, pomp, and fertility to a desert.
Go beyond a certain point of restitution, and to
restore is to destroy.   Every great literary age
with us has been that in which the language
has the most largely borrowed from the spirit
of some foreign tongue—a startling proposition,
but borne out by facts.   The spirit of Ancient
Letters passing into our language, as yet virgin
of all offspring, begat literature itself.  In Elizabeth's day, besides Greek and Latin, we borrowed most largely from the Italian.   The
genius of that day is Italian poetry transfused,
and sublimed by the transition, into a rougher
tongue.   In the reign of Queen Anne we were
equally indebted to the French, and nothing
can be more Gallic than the prose of Addison
and the verse of Pope.   In the day imme-

diately preceding our own, besides returning
to our old writers, viz. the borrowers from the
Italian and French, we have caught much of
the moonlight and dreamy character of romance
— much of the mingled chivalry and mysticism
that marked the favourite productions of the
time, from the masterpieces of Germany.* In
fact, I suspect that every great writer of a
nation a little corrupts its tongue. His knowledge suggests additions and graces from other
tongues; his genius applies and makes them
popular. Milton was the greatest poet of our
country, and there is scarcely an English idiom
which he has not violated, or a foreign one
which he has not borrowed. Voltaire accuses

* It is not often very easy to trace the manner in which
an author is indebted to the spirit of a foreign literature,
and which he may not even know in the original. Wordsworth, Coleridge, and Scott, knew German, and their
knowledge is manifest in their own writings. Byron was
unacquainted with German; yet he was deeply imbued
with the German intellectual spirit. A vast number of
German fictions had been translated at the beginning of
the century. They ran the round of the circulating libraries,
and coloured and prepared the minds of the ordinary reading public, unknowingly to themselves, for the favourable
reception of the first English writer in a similar school.
I have heard from a relation of Byron's, that he had read
these fictions largely in his youth, and that which swayed
his mind in its cast of sentiment, laid the train in the general mind for the effect that he produced.

the simple La Fontaine of having corrupted the language; the same charge was made against Voltaire himself. Rousseau was yet more open to the accusation than Voltaire. Chateaubriand and De Stael are the corruptors of the style of Rousseau, and Courier has grafted new licences on the liberties arrogated by Voltaire. Nothing could be more simple and unpretending than the style of Scott, yet he is perpetually accused of having tainted the purity of our idioms; so that the language may be said to acquire its chief triumphs by those who seem the least to have paid deference to its forms.

It is some comfort, amidst the declamations of Starch, to think that the system of intellectual commerce with foreign languages is somewhat like the more vulgar trade, and if it corrupts, must be allowed at least to enrich.

You know, my dear sir, that in France, that lively country, where they always get up a dispute for the amusement of the spectators,—where the nobles encouraged a democracy, for the pleasurable excitement of the controversy; and religion itself has been played like a game at shuttlecock, which is lost the moment the antagonists cease their blows;—in France, the good people still divert themselves with disputing the several merits of the Classical School, and the Romantic. They have the two schools—*that* is certain — let us be permitted to question the excellence of the scholars in either.

The English have not disputed on the matter, and the consequence is, that their writers have contrived to amalgamate the chief qualities of *both* schools. Thus, the style of Byron is at once classical and romantic ; and, the Edinburgh reviewers have well observed, may please either a Gifford or a Shelley. And even a Shelley, whom some would style emphatically of the Romantic School, has formed himself on the model of the Classic. His genius is eminently Greek : he has become romantic, by being peculiarly classical.*

Thus while the two schools abroad have been declaring an union incompatible, we have united them quietly, without saying a word on the matter. Heaven only knows to what extremes of absurdity we should have gone in the spirit of emulation, if we had thought fit to set up a couple of parties, to prove which was best ! †

* This observation will extend even to Keates himself, the last of the new school. ' Endymion' and ' Saturn' are both modelled from the casts of antiquity.

† The question of the difference between the Romantic School and the Classic, has been merely that of forms.

What, in the name of common sense, signify disputes about
the Unities and such stuff,—the ceremonies of the Muses?
The Medea would have been equally Greek if all the unities had been disregarded. The Faust equally romantic,
if all the unities had been preserved. It is among the
poems of Homer and Pindar, of Æschylus and Hesiod,
that you must look for the spirit of antiquity; but these
gentlemen look to the rules of Aristotle: it is as if a sculp-
tor, instead of studying the statue of the Apollo, should
study the yard measure that takes its proportions.

# CHAPTER V.

## THE DRAMA.

The Public do not always pay for their Amusement—The State of the
French Theatre—The French Drama murders and the English robs
—Vulgar Plagiarism from the old Dramatists—Jack Old Crib—The Influence of the Laws—Want of able Dramas but not of dramatic Talent—
Should Political Allusions be banished from the Stage?—Inquiry into
what should be the true Sources of Dramatic Interest—The Simple
and the Magnificent—The Simple considered—Kings no longer the
fitting agents of the Tragic emotion—Antient Rules of Tragic Criticism
are therefore not applicable to Modern Times—Second 'Source of Dramatic Interest—The Magnificent considered—In Melo-drame are the
Seeds of the new Tragedy, as in Ballads lay the Seeds of Modern
Poetry.

" ONE may always leave the amusements to
the care of the public; they are sure to pay for
*those* well:" thus said a mathematician to me,
the other day, with the air of a man who wished
benevolently to insinuate, that one made too
much by one's novels, and that the king ought
to give such a good mathematician as he was,
five thousand a year at the least.

"The deuce you may, sir!—What then do
you say to the drama?—Actors, authors, mana-

gers, singers, painters, jugglers, lions from My-
sore, and elephants from Siam, all are working
night and day to amuse you.  And I fancy that
the theatres are nevertheless but a poor speculation."

" Yes, but in this country — monopoly ;  no
protection to the authors — theatres too big,—
free trade," mumbled the mathematician.

" Certainly, you are quite right—but look to
France.  No legislature can be more polite to
the drama, than is the legislature of France.
Authors protected, a Dramatic Board, plenty of
theatres, no censor; and yet the poor Drama is in
a very bad way even there.  The Government are
forced to allow the theatres several thousands a
year ; without that assistance they would be shut
up.  Messieurs the Public pay something to
the piper, but not all the requisite salary ;  so
that you see it is not quite true, that the public
will always pay well for their own amusements."

If this be the case in France, I fear it must be
still more the case in England.  For in France,
amusement is a necessary, while here it is scarcely
even a luxury.  " L'amusement est un des be-
soins de l'homme," said Voltaire.  *Oui, Monsieur
de Voltaire,—de l'homme François!* In England,
thanks to our taxes, we have not yet come to
reckon amusements among our *absolute* wants.

But everywhere throughout Europe the glory of the theatre is beginning to grow dim, as if there were certain arts in the world which blaze and have their day, and then die off in silence and darkness, like an exhausted volcano. In France it is not only that the theatre is not prosperous, but that, with every advantage and stimulus, the talent for the theatre is degenerate. The French authors have started a new era in Art, by putting an end to Nature. They now try only to write something eccentric. They want to excite terror, by showing you bugbears that cannot exist. When Garrick wished to awe you, he had merely to change the expression of his countenance; a child wishing to terrify you, puts on a mask. The French authors put on a mask.

The French dramatists have now pretty nearly run through the whole catalogue of out-of-the-way crimes, and when that is completed, there will be an end of their materials. After the *Tour de Nesle*, what more can they think of in the way of atrocity? In this play, the heroine poisons her father, stabs and drowns all the lovers she can get (number unknown); intrigues with one son, and assassinates the other! After such a selection from the fair sex it is difficult to guess, from what female conception of the

Beautiful the French Poets will form their next fashionable heroine!

The French Theatre is wretched; it has been made the field for the two schools to fight in, and the combatants have left all their dead bodies on the stage.

If the French Theatre lives upon murders, the English exists upon robberies; it steals every thing it can lay its hands upon; to-day it filches a French farce, to-morrow it becomes sacrilegious, and commits a burglary on the Bible. The most honest of our writers turn up their noses at the rogues who steal from foreigners, and with a spirit of lofty patriotism confine their robberies to the literature of their own country. These are they, who think that to steal old goods is no theft: they are the brokers of books, and their avowed trade is second-hand. They hunt among the Heywoods and Deckers, pillage a plot from Fletcher or Shirley; and as for their language, they steal *that* everywhere; these are they who fill every page with "go to" and "peradventure." If a lady asks her visiters to be seated, it is

> "Pray ye, sit down, good gentles;"

if a lover admires the fashion of his mistress's gown;—she answereth:—

> "Ay, by my faith, 'tis quaint!"

if a gentleman complains of a wound,

> " It shall be look'd to, sir, right heedfully."

A dramatic author of this nature is the very Autolycus of plagiarists; "an admirable conceited fellow, and hath ribbons of all the colours of the rainbow;" he sayeth, indeed, that he derives *assistance only* from the elder dramatists— he robbeth not; no! *he catcheth the spirit!* verily this he doth all in the true genius of Autolycus, when he assists himself with the Clown, as thus :—

### CLOWN.

How now!   Canst stand?

### AUTOLYCUS.

Softly, dear Sir, (*picks his pocket :*) good Sir, softly. You ha' done me a charitable office.

Jack Old-Crib is a dramatic author of this class; you never heard a man so bitter against the frivolity of those who filch from the French vaudevilles. Their want of magnanimity displeases him sadly. He is mightily bitter on the success of Tom Fribble, who lives by translating one-act farces from Scribe; he calls *that* plagiarism: meanwhile, Jack Old-Crib steals with all the loftiness of a five-act poet, and, worse than Fribble—does not even acknowledge the offence. No; he steals plot, character, diction and all, from Dodsley's Col-

lection, but calls *that*, with a majestic smile,
" reviving the Antient Drama."

Certainly there have been many reasons for
the present deterioration of dramatic literature
to be ascribed solely to the state of the laws.
In the first place, what men that can write popularly anything else, would write for the stage, so
long as, while they were damned if they might
fail, they could get nothing if they succeeded?
Does any fruit, even a crab-apple, flourish in
that land where there is no security for property? The drama has been that land.   In
the second place,  the two large theatres, having
once gorged the public with show, have rendered themselves unfit  for  dignified  comedy
and  sober  entertainments, because  they have
created  a  public  unfit  to  relish  them.   The
minor  theatres  exhibit  against  the  law,  few
persons  of  capital  are  disposed  to  embark
property  in illegal speculations.   The sites of
many of these theatres, too, are ill-chosen, and
the  audience  not  sufficiently  guided  in  their
tastes  by  persons of literary refinement.   Some
of  these  evils  we  may  hope  to  reform.   You
know, sir, that I have introduced into Parliament  two bills, one of which will  give  protection to authors, and  the  other  encourage competition in theatres.   The first has received the
royal assent, and  become law.   I  trust for the

same good fortune for the second.*   Doubtless
these improvements in legislation may be ex-
tremely beneficial in their ultimate consequences.

But there are causes of deterioration which
the law cannot control ; and, looking to the
state of the drama abroad, while our experiment ought to be adventured, we must confess
its success to be doubtful.  Still more doubtful is it when we recollect that, if the state
of the law were the only cause of the deterioration of the drama, by removing the cause
you cannot always remove the effect which the
cause has engendered.  The public being once
spoiled by show, it is not easy to bring them
back to a patient love of chaste composition.  The public, also, being once rendered
indifferent to the drama, it is not easy to restore the taste.  " Tardiora sunt remedia quàm
mala, et, ut corpora lente augescunt, cito exstin-
guuntur, sic ingenia studiaque oppresseris, fa-
cilius quàm revocaris."  A very profound remark, which means simply that when the Drama
has once gone to the dogs, it will be a matter
of time to heal the marks of their teeth.  It is
easier to create a taste than to revive one.  Most
of us, how simple men soever, can beget life

* Since the first edition of this work, the Bill here referred to
has been lost in the Lords, after having passed the Commons by
a majority of four to one.   Very well !—We must try again.

without any extraordinary exertion ; but it
requires a very able physician to restore the
dying.   At present let us remove the obstacles
to the operations of nature, and trust that *she*
will be the physician at last.   And, at least, we
must admit that the present age has shown no
lack of dramatic talent.  Of dramatic talent suited to *the taste of the day*, it assuredly has ; but
not of dramatic talent examined by the criteria
of high art.   I have already spoken of the
magnificent tragedies of Byron : I may add to
those the stern and terrible conception of the
Cençi.   Nor ought we to forget the Mirandola
of Barry Cornwall, or the Evadne of Sheil—
both works that, if written at an earlier period,
would have retained a permanent and high station on the stage.   The plays of Mr. Knowles,
though at one time overlauded by the critics,
and somewhat perhaps disfigured by imitations
of the elder dramatists, testify considerable
mastery of effect, and, with the exception of
Victor Hugo's *chef-d'œuvres*, are undeniably
superior to the contemporaneous dramas of
France.

   The greater proportion of prose fictions with
us, too, have been written by the dramatic rules,
rather than the epic, and evince an amplitude
of talent for the stage, had their authors been

POLITICS BANISHED FROM THE STAGE. 141

encouraged so to apply it. In fine, then, the theatre wants good dramas; but the age shows no want of dramatic ability. Let us hope for the best, but not expect too speedy a realization of the hope. The political agitation of the times is peculiarly unfavourable to the arts: when people are busy, they are not eager to be amused. The great reason why the Athenians, always in a sea of politics, were nevertheless always willing to crowd the theatre, was this—*the theatre with them was political;* tragedy embodied the sentiment, and comedy represented the characters, of the times. Thus theatrical performance was to the Athenian a newspaper as well as a play. We banish the Political from the stage, and we therefore deprive the stage of the most vivid of its actual sources of interest. At present the English, instead of finding politics on the stage, find their stage in politics. In the testimony of the witnesses examined before the Dramatic Committee, it is universally allowed that a censor is not required to keep immorality from the stage, but to prevent political allusions. I grant that in too great a breadth of political allusions there is a certain mischief: politics addressed to the people should not come before the tribunal of their imagina-

tion, but that of their reason ; in the one
you only excite by convincing—in the other
you begin at the wrong end, and convince
by exciting. At the same time, I doubt if
the drama will become thoroughly popular
until it is permitted to embody the most popular emotions. In these times the public mind
is absorbed in politics, and yet the stage,
which should represent the times, especially
banishes appeals to the most general feelings.
To see our modern plays, you would imagine
there were no politicians among us: the national theatre, to use a hacknied but appropriate jest, is like the play of Hamlet " with
the part of Hamlet left out by the particular
desire"——of the nobility !

But as the censor will be retained, and
politics will still be banished from the stage, let
us endeavour to content ourselves with the great
benefits that, ere the end of another year, I trust
we shall have effected for the advancement of
the Stage. By the one law already enacted,
authors will have nothing material to complain
of ; a successful and standard play, bestowing
on them some emolument every time it is performed, will be a source of permanent income.
Some of the best writers of the age (for the
best are often the poorest) will therefore be

encouraged to write plays, and to write not for the hour only, but for permanent fame. By the second law, which I trust will soon be passed, every theatre will be permitted to act the legitimate drama : there will therefore be no want of competition in the number of theatres, no just ground of complaint as to their dispro- portionate size. There will be theatres enough, and theatres of all dimensions. I imagine the two large theatres will, however, continue to be the most important and influential. Monopoly misguided their efforts,—emulation will rectify the direction. These are great reforms. Let us make the most of them, and see, if despite the languor of the drama abroad, we cannot revive its national vigour at home.

And to effect this restauration, let us examine what are the true sources of dramatic interest which belong to this age. Let us borrow the divining rod, and see to what new fountains it will lead us.

Heaven and yourself, dear sir, know how many years ago it is since the members of the poetical world cried out, " Let us go back to the old poets." Back to the old poets accord- ingly they went—the inspiration revived them. Poetry bathed in the youth of the language, and became once more young. But the most

sacred inspiration never lasts above a generation
or two, and the power of achieving wonders
wears itself out after the death of the first disciples.  Just when the rest of the literary
world began to think the new poets had made
quite enough out of the old, just when they
had grown weary of transfusing the spirit of
chivalry and ballads into the genius of modern
times, just when they had begun to allow that
what was a good thing once, was beginning to
grow too much of a good thing now, up starts
our friend the Drama, with the wise look of a
man who has suddenly perceived the meaning of
a *bon mot*, that all the rest of the company have
already admired and done with, and says, " Go
back to the old poets.  What an excellent
idea !  The Drama, which ought to be the first
intellectual representative to reflect every important change in the literary spirit of the
world, has with us been the last, and is now going back to Elizabeth's day for an inspiration
which a more alert species of poetry has already exhausted of the charm of freshness.
It seizes on what is most hacknied, and an-
nounces its treasure as most new.  When we
are all palled with the *bon mot*, it begins to din
it into our ears as a capital new story.  This
will never do.  To revive the Stage we must

now go forward, the golden bridge behind us
is broken down by the multitude of passengers
who have crossed it.   The darkness closes once
more over the lovely Spirit of the departed
Poetry, and like the fairy of her own wells and
waterfalls, the oftener she has revisited the earth,
the fainter has become her beauty, and the less
powerful her charm.

> " Like to a child o'erwearied with sweet toil,
>     On its own folded wings and wavy hair
>     The spirit of the earth is laid asleep !"

There are two sources from which we should
now seek the tragic influence, viz. the Simple
and the Magnificent.  Tales of a household
nature, that find their echo in the hearts of the
people — the materials of the village tragedy,
awaking an interest common to us all ; intense
yet homely, actual — earnest — the pathos and
passion of every-day life ; such as the stories of
Jeannie Deans or of Carwell, in prose fiction ;—
behold one great source of those emotions to
which the dramatic author of this generation
ought to apply his genius !  Originally the
personages of tragedy were rightly taken
from the great.  With a just propriety, Kings
stalked the scenic boards ; the heroine was
a queen, the lover a warrior : —*for in those
days there was no people!*  Emotions were

VOL. II.

supposed to be more tragic in proportion as the station of their victims was elevated. This notion was believed in common life, and to represent it was therefore natural and decorous to the Stage. But we have now learnt another faith in the actual world, and to that faith, if we desire to interest the spectator, we must appeal upon the stage. We have learnt to consider that emotions are *not* the most passionately experienced in a court; that the feelings of Kings are not more intense than those of persons who are more roused by the stern excitements of life, nor the passions of a Queen less freed from frivolity, than the maiden of humbler fortunes, who loves from the depths of a heart which hath no occupation but love. We know the great now as persons assuredly whom it is wise and fitting to respect; incarnations of the august ceremonies in which a nation parades its own grandeur and pleases its own pride. For my part I do not profess a vulgar intolerance of belief that Kings must be worse than other men;* but we know at least,

---

* Nay, if they were so, they would be—terrible scourges, it is true, to the world — but *quelque chose de bon* for the Stage. It really is because Kings are now so rarely guilty of gigantic crime, that they cease to awe and terrify us on the Stage.

amidst a round of forms, and an etiquette of
frivolities, that their souls cannot be so large,
nor their passions so powerful, nor their emotions so intensely tragic as those of men in whom
the active enterprises of life constantly stimulate the desires and nerve the powers. The
passions are the elements of tragedy. Whatever renders the passions weak and regulated is
serviceable to morals, and unfitted for the Stage.
A good man who never sins against reason is
an excellent character, but a tame hero. But
morals alone do not check the passions ; frivolities check them also. And the nature of a King
is controlled and circumscribed to limits too
narrow for the Tragic, (which demands excess,)
not perhaps by the virtues that subdue, but the
ceremonies which restrain, him. Kings of old
were the appropriate heroes of the stage ; for all
the vastest of human ideas circled and enshrined
them. The heroic and the early Christian age
alike agreed in attributing to the Crowned Head
a mysterious and solemn sanctity. Delegates
of supernatural agents, they were the gods or
dæmons of the earth ; the hearts of mankind
were compelled to a dread and irresistible interest in their actions. They were the earthly
repositories of human fate ; when their representatives appeared upon the stage, habited

and attended as *they* were, it was impossible that the interest of the spectator, so highly wrought at the reality, should not be prepared to transfer itself to the likeness. Then indeed that interest itself assumed a grand and tragic dignity. What vivid and awful emotions must those have experienced who surveyed the fate of beings who were the arch dispensers of the fates themselves ! *

The belief which attached to a Sovereign something of the power and the sanctity of a god, necessarily beheld a superhuman dignity in his love, and a terrible sublimity in his woe. The misfortunes that happened to the monarch were as punishments upon the people ; the spectators felt themselves involved in the consequences of his triumph or his fall. Thus kings were the most appropriate heroes of the tragic muse, because their very appearance on the stage appealed to the Sublime—the superstition of the beholder stamped a gigantic grandeur on the august sufferer—and united with the pathos of human interest the awe of religion itself. The habits of monarchy in the elder age strengthened this delusion. For both in the remote classic and the later feudal time, the

---

* " Princes are like to heavenly bodies, which cause good or evil times."—BACON.

people did not represent themselves so much
as they were represented in their chief. And
when Shakspeare introduces Henry V. upon
the stage, the spectators beheld not a king only,
but the type of their own triumphs — the
breathing personification of the trophies of Agin-
court, and the abasement of France. To add
yet more to the interest that encircled the
tragic hero — the people, as I have just said,
were *not*—Wisdom, Education, and Glory were
alike the monopoly of the great. Then knowledge had nòt taught to the mass of mankind
the mighty sources of interest which lay, un-
touched by the poet, in their own condition.
The popular heart was only known in its great
convulsions — it was the high-born and the
knightly who were alone represented as faithful
in love—generous in triumph—and magna-
nimous in adversity. The people were painted
as a mob — fickle, insolent, and cruel ; perhaps
in that state of civilization they were nothing
more. It may be that the great, being the best
educated, were really the noblest part of the
community.

In former times then, there were reasons
which do not exist at present—that rendered
the Great the fitting heroes of the tragic stage.
Kings do not awaken the same awful and mys-

terious emotions that they once inspired—if
not without the theatre, neither will they within
its walls.   You may go back to the old time,
you may present to us an Œdipus or an Aga-
memnon, a Richard or a Henry; but you will
not revive in us the same feelings with which
their representatives were once beheld.   Our
reason tacitly allows that these names were
clothed with associations different from those
which surround modern Sovereigns.   But our
feelings do not obey our reason — we cannot
place ourselves in the condition of those who
would have felt their blood thrill as the crowned
shadows moved across the stage.   We cannot
fill our bosoms with the emotions that sleep in
the dust of our departed fathers.   We gaze
upon the purple of past kings with the irre-
verent apathy of modern times.   Kings are no
longer Destinies.   And the interest they excited
has departed with their power.   Whither?—to
the People!   Among the people, then, must the
tragic author invoke the genius of Modern
Tragedy, and learn its springs.

If this principle be true, down falls at once
all the old fabric of criticism upon the tragic
art!   Down falls the pile of reasonings built to
tell us why Kings, Princesses, Generals, and
" the nobility in general" must be the characters

of a true tragedy ! Down go the barriers which so rigidly shut out from the representation of ele-vated nature—the classes in which her elements are the most impassioned and their operations the most various ! A new order of things has arisen in the actual world, and the old rules* in-stituted for the purpose of illustrating the actual world by the ideal, crumble to the dust !

In Shelley's noble thought, the Spirit of Power and Poesy passes into the Universal Heart :

> " It interpenetrates the granite mass ;—"

beings are called forth " less mighty but more mild," and

> " Familiar acts grow beautiful through Love !"

The SIMPLE, then, is one legitimate (and I hold the *principal*) source of the modern tragedy—its materials being woven from the woes—the passions—the various and multiform

---

* I grant that the stage must not only represent but en-noble Nature—its likenesses must be spiritualized ; but this it can effect equally from whatever grade its characters are drawn. Clarissa Harlowe is taken from the middle ranks —could the character of any queen have been more spiri-tualized ? Goldsmith's Country Clergyman is nature—but nature ennobled. Faust is a German scholar ; but par-takes more largely of the grand ideal than any Prince (save Hamlet) idealized by the magic of Shakspeare himself.

characters—that are to be found in the different grades of an educated and highly civilized people;—materials a thousand times more rich, subtle, and complex, than those sought only in the region of royal existence, the paucity of which we may perceive by the monotonous sameness of the characters into which, in the regal tragedy, they are moulded. The eternal prince, and his eternal confidant; the ambitious traitor, and the jealous tyrant; the fair captive, and her female friend!—we should not have had these *dramatis personæ* so often, if authors had not conceived themselves limited to the intrigues, the events, and the creations of a court.

Another and totally distinct source of modern tragedy may be sought in the MAGNIFICENT. True art never rejects the materials which are within its reach. The Stage has gained a vast acquisition in pomp and show—utterly unknown to any period of its former history. The most elaborate devices of machinery, the most exquisite delusions of scene, may indeed be said to snatch us

" From Thebes to Athens when and where you will."

The public have grown wedded to this magnificence. Be it so. Let the dramatist effect, then, what Voltaire did under a similar passion

of the public, and * marry the scenic pomp " to
immortal verse." Instead of abusing and carping
at the public for liking the more gorgeous attractions, be it the task of our dramatists to elevate
the attractions themselves. Let them borrow
all they can from the sister arts, (in this they
have the advantage of other poets, who must
depend on the one art alone,) but let them
make their magnificent allies subservient to the
one great art they profess. In short, let
them employ an equal gorgeousness of effect ;
but instead of wasting it on a spectacle, or a
melodrame, make it instrumental to the achievements of tragedy herself. The astonishing
richness and copiousness of modern stage illu-
sion opens to the poet a mighty field, which his
predecessors could not enter. For him are indeed " the treasures of earth, and air, and sea."
The gorgeous Ind with her mighty forests and
glittering spires ; " Fanatic Egypt and her
priests ;" the stern superstitions of the North
—its wizard pine-glens—its hills of snow and
lucid air

    " Clad in the beauty of a thousand stars:—"

---

  * Helvetius complains, however, that in his day, their
full effect could not be given to magnificence and display,
on account of the fashion of the spectators to crowd the
stage.

whatever Nature hath created, whatever history hath bequeathed, whatever fancy can devise
—all now are within the power of the artist to
summon upon the Stage. The poet of the
drama hath no restrictions on his imagination from the deficiency of skill to embody
corporeally his creations, and that which the
epic poet can only describe by words, the
tragic poet can fix into palpable and visible
life. The MAGNIFICENT, then, is the second
source of modern dramatic inspiration, combining all the attractions of scenery, embracing
the vastest superstitions and most glowing
dreams of an unbounded imagination. We
may see that these two are the real sources of
modern dramatic art, by the evidence, that even
performances below the mediocre which have
resorted to either source, have been the most
successful with the public,— have struck the
most powerfully on the sentiment of the age.
The play of " The Gamblers," or " The
Soldier's Wife," or of " Clari," or " The Maid
and the Magpie"—all, however differing each
from each, partake of the one attribute of the
popular or domestic tragedy ; and though of a
very inferior order of poetical talent, invariably excite a vivid emotion in the audience.
So, on the other hand, the splendour of an Easter

spectacle, or the decorations of an almost panto-
mimic melodrame, produce an admiration which
wins forgiveness to the baldness of the dialogue
and the absurdity of the plot. How then would
performances of either class attract, supposing
their effect were aided by proportionate skill in
the formation of character, the melody of language, and the conception of design;—by the
witchery of a true poet, and the execution of a
consummate artist! Not then by pondering over
inapplicable rules,—not by recurring to past
models,—not by recasting hacknied images, but
by a bold and masterly adaptation of modern
materials to modern taste, will an author revive
the glories of the drama. In this, he will in
reality profit by the study of Shakspeare, who
addressed *his* age, and so won the future. He
will do as all the master-minds of his own day
have done in other regions of poetry. Byron
and Scott, Göthe and Schiller, all took the
germ of a popular impulse, and breathed into it
a finished and glorious life, by the spirit of their
own genius. Instead of decrying the public
opinion which first manifested itself in a love for
the lower and more frivolous portion of a certain
taste, those great masters cultivated that taste to
the highest, and so at once conciliated and exalted the public mind. What the ballads of

Monk Lewis were to Scott, the melodrames, whether simple or gorgeous, should be to the future Scott of the drama.

A true genius, however elevated, is refreshed by the streams that intersect the popular heart, just as, by the mysterious attraction of Nature, high peaks and mountains draw up, through a thousand invisible tubes, the waters that play amidst the plains below !

# CHAPTER VI.

## MORAL PHILOSOPHY.

Each great movement has its philosophy—The philosophy of our time
is that of the Economists—Moralists not silenced but affected by the tone
of general speculative research—Ours are therefore of the material
school—Bailey—Mill—Hazlitt—Bentham—Character of Bentham's
Philosophy, &c.—Bentham greater as a Legislator than Moralist—
Insufficiency of the greatest happiness principle—Singular that no
ideal school has sprung up amongst us—Professorships the best means
to advance those studies which the Public cannot reward.

EVERY great Movement in a civilized age has
its reflection—that reflection is the Philosophy
of the period. The Movement which in England commenced by the Church Reformation,
and slowly progressed during the reign of
Elizabeth and James, till it acquired energy
for the gigantic impulse and mighty rush of
the Republican Revolution, had (as the consequence of the *one* part of its progress, and the
prophet of the *other*)—its great philosophical
representative—in the profound, inquisitive,
and innovating soul of Bacon. The Movement

which restored Charles II. to the throne, which
filled the Court—whose threshold had been so
lately darkened by the sombre majesty of Crom-
well—with men without honour and women
without shame—demanded a likeness of itself;
it exacted its own philosophy; a moral mirror
of the growing reaction from the turbulence
of a fanatical freedom to the lethargy and base
contentment of a profligate despotism;—a system that should invent slavery as the standard
of legislation, and selfishness as the criterion of
morals:—that philosophy, that reflection, and
that system, had their representative in Hobbes.
The Leviathan which charmed the Court, and
was even studied by the King, was the moral of
the Restoration—it embodied the feelings that
first produced and afterwards coloured that
event.   A sterner era advanced.   A bolder
thought demanded a new likeness—the Movement advanced from the Restoration to the
Revolution—the Movement once more required
its philosophy, and received that philosophy in
Locke.   In his mind lay the type of the sentiments that produced the Revolution—in his
philosophy, referring all things to Reason only,
its voice was heard.   As diverted from the
theory of governments—the Spirit of Research
was stimulated by a multiplied and encreasing

commerce, as the middle class increased into power; and the activity of Trade, disdaining the theories of the closet, demanded a philosophy for the mart; a more extensive if less visible Movement in civilization, required also its reflection, and the representative of the new movement was the author of the Wealth of Nations.

Each philosophy, vast and profound enough to represent its epoch, endures for a certain time, and entails upon us a succession of spirits more or less brilliant, that either by attacking or defending, by imitating, or illustrating that peculiar philosophy, continue its influential prevalence amongst us for a longer or shorter period — when at last it darkens away from the actual and outer world, banished like the scenes of a by-gone play from the glare of the lamps and the gaze of the audience, falling into the silence of neglected lumber, and replaced by some new system, which a new necessity of the age has called into existence. We as yet live under the influence of the philosophy of Adam Smith. The minds that formerly would have devoted themselves to metaphysical and moral research, are given up to inquiries into a more material study. Political economy replaces ethics; and we have treatises on the theory of rents, instead of essays on the theory of motives. It is the age of political economists; and while we see with regret the lamp of a purer naphtha almost entirely extinct in England, we must confess that foreigners have been unjust to us when they contend that for the last half century we have been producing little or nothing to the service of the human mind.—We have produced Ricardo!—When they accuse us of the want of speculative industry, let us confront them with the pamphlets upon pamphlets that issue monthly from the press, upon speculative points alone. As in the three celebrated springs in Iceland, the stream rushes at once into one only, leaving the others dry; so the copiousness of investigation upon Political Science, leaves exhausted and unrefreshed the fountains of Metaphysics and of Ethics. The spirit of the age demands political economy now, as it demanded moral theories before. Whoever will desire to know hereafter the character of our times, must find it in the philosophy of the Economists.

But the influence of a prevailing monopoly of speculative inquiry, while it deadens the general tendency towards the other branches of intellectual commerce, cannot wholly silence the few devoted and earnest minds which refuse to follow in the common current, and pursue apart and alone their independent meditations. It cannot silence—but I apprehend it will *affect* them ;—the fashion of materialism in one branch of inquiry will materialize the thought that may be exercised in another. Thus all our *few* recent English moralists are of the Material School. Not touching now upon the *Scotch* schools, from which the spirit of Adam Smith has (comparatively speaking) passed, and grown naturalized with us ; nor commenting on the beautiful philosophizing rather than philosophy of Dugald Stewart—the most exquisite critic upon the systems of others that our language has produced—fulfilling to philosophy the office that Schlegel fulfilled to literature,—I shall just point out, in my way to the most celebrated moralist of the time, the few that have dignified similar pursuits. Mr. Bailey of Sheffield, has produced some graceful speculations upon Truth, and the Formati of Opinions, written in a liberal spirit and a style of peculiar purity. Mr. Mill has, in a work of remarkable acuteness, but written in so compressed and Spartan a form that to abridge it would be almost to anatomize a skeleton — followed out certain theories of Hartley into a new analysis of the Human Mind. His work requires a minute and painful study — it partakes of the severe logic of his more famous treatises on Government and Education ; it is the *only* purely metaphysical book attracting any notice, which to my knowledge has been published in England for the last fifteen years.*

Mr. Hazlitt has also left behind him an early work, entitled " An Essay on the Principles of Human Action ;" little known, and rarely to be met with, but full of original remarks, and worthy a diligent perusal.†

In the science of Jurisprudence, Mr. Austen has thrown considerable light upon many intricate questions, and has illustrated a sterile subject with passages of a lofty eloquence — another proof, be it observed, of the value of Professorships ;— the work is the republication of lectures, and might never have been composed

---

* See some additional remarks upon this eminent writer in Appendix C.

† I do not here comment on the writings of Mr. Godwin ; they belong, in their character and their influence, rather to the last century than the present. Mr. Hope (the author of Anastasius) left behind him a philosophical work, which has since been suppressed—it may be difficult to say whether the style or the sense of it be the less worthy the fine genius of the author. Lady Mary Shepherd has shown no ordinary acuteness in her Essay upon " The Relation of Cause and Effect."

in these days, but for the *necessity* of composing it.

But in legislative and moral philosophy, Bentham must assuredly be considered the most celebrated and influential teacher of the age—a master, indeed, whom few have acknowledged, but from whom thousands have, mediately and unconsciously, imbibed their opinions.

The same causes which gave so great a fertility to the school of the Economists, had their effect upon the philosophy of Bentham; they drew his genius mainly towards examinations of men rather than of man—of the defects of Law, and of the hypocrisies and fallacies of our Social System; they contributed to the material form and genus of his code, and to those notions of Utility which he considered his own invention, but which had been incorporated with half the systems that had risen in Europe since the sensualism of Condillac had been grafted upon the reflection of Locke. But causes far more latent, and perhaps more powerful, contributed also to form the mind and philosophy of Bentham. He had preceded the great French Revolution—the materials of his thoughts had been compounded from the same foundations of opinion as those on which the more enlightened advocates of the Revo-

lution would have built up that edifice which
was to defy a second deluge, and which is but
a record of the confusion of the workmen.
With the philosophy of the eighteenth century,
which first adopted what the French reasoners
term the Principle of Humanity—(that is, the
principle of philanthropy—a paramount regard
for multitudes rather than for sectarian interests,)—with this philosophy, I say, the whole
mind of Bentham was imbued and saturate.
He had no mercy, no toleration for the knots
and companies of men whom he considered in-
terrupters or monopolists of the power of the
many — to his mind they were invariably actuated by base and designing motives, and such
motives, according to his philosophy, they were
even *compelled* to entertain.   His intellect was
as the aqueduct which bore aloft, and over the
wastes and wrecks below, the stream of the
philosophy of one century to the generations
of the other.   His code of morals, original in
its results, is in many parts (unconsciously
to himself) an eclecticism of nearly all the best
parts of the various theories of a century.   "The
system of Condillac required its '*moral*' code,
and Helvetius supplied it."   The moral code of
Helvetius required its legislative, and in Bentham it obtained it.   I consider, then, that two

series of causes conspired to produce Bentham
—the one national, the other belonging to all
Europe; the same causes on the one hand
which produced with us the Economists—the
same causes on the other hand which produced
in France, Helvetius and Diderot, Volney, Con-
dorcet, and Voltaire. He combined what had
not been yet done, the spirit of the Philanthro-
pic with that of the Practical. He did not
declaim about abuses; he went at once to their
root: he did not idly penetrate the sophistries
of Corruption; he smote Corruption herself.
He was the very Theseus of legislative reform,
—he not only pierced the labyrinth—he destroyed the monster.

As he drew his vigour from the stream of
Change, all his writings tended to their original
source. He collected from the Past the scattered remnants of a defeated innovation, and led
them on against the Future. Every age may be
called an age of transition—the passing on, as it
were, from one state to another never ceases;
but in our age the transition is *visible*, and
Bentham's philosophy is the philosophy of a
visible transition. Much has already happened,
much is already happening every instant, in
this country—throughout Europe—throughout
the world, which might not have occurred if

Bentham had not been; yet of all his works,
none have been read by great numbers; and
most of them, from their difficulties of style and
subject, have little chance of ever being generally popular. He acted upon the destinies of
his race by influencing the thoughts of a minute
fraction of the few who think—from them the
broad principles travelled onward—became
known—(their source unknown)—became familiar and successful. I have said that we live in
an age of visible transition—an age of disquietude and doubt—of the removal of time-worn
landmarks, and the breaking up of the hereditary elements of society—old opinions, feelings
—ancestral customs and institutions are crum-
bling away, and both the spiritual and tempo-
ral worlds are darkened by the shadow of
change. The commencement of one of these
epochs—periodical in the history of mankind—
is hailed by the sanguine as the coming of a
new Millennium—a great iconoclastic reformation, by which all false gods shall be over-
thrown. To me such epochs appear but as the
dark passages in the appointed progress of mankind—the times of greatest unhappiness to our
species—passages into which we have no reason
to rejoice at our entrance, save from the hope
of being sooner landed on the opposite side.

Uncertainty is the greatest of all our evils. And I know of no happiness where there is not a firm unwavering belief in its duration.

The age then is one of *destruction!* disguise it as we will, it must be so characterized; miserable would be our lot were it not also an age of preparation for reconstructing. What has been the influence of Bentham upon his age?—it has been twofold — he has helped to destroy and also to rebuild. No one has done so much to forward, at least in this country, the work of destruction, as Mr. Bentham. The spirit of examination and questioning has become through him, more than through any one person besides, the prevailing spirit of the age. For he questioned all things. The tendencies of a mind at once sceptical and systematic, (and both in the utmost possible degree,) made him endeavour to trace all speculative phenomena back to their primitive elements, and to reconsider not only the received conclusions, but the received premises. He treated all subjects as if they were virgin subjects, never before embraced or approached by man. He did not set up an established doctrine as a thesis to be disputed about, but put it aside altogether, commenced from first principles, and deliberately tasked himself systematically to discover the truth, or to re-discover it if it were already known.   By this process, if he ever annihilated a received opinion, he was sure of having something either good or bad to offer as a substitute for it; and in this he was most favourably distinguished from those French philosophers who preceded and even surpassed him, as destroyers of established institutions on the continent of Europe.   And we shall owe largely to one who reconstructed while he destroyed, if our country is destined to pass more smoothly through this crisis of transition than the nations of the Continent, and to lose less of the good it already enjoys in working itself free from the evil;—his be the merit, if while the wreck of the old vessel is still navigable, the masts of the new one, which brings relief, are dimly showing themselves above the horizon!   For it is certain, and will be seen every day more clearly, that the initiation of all the changes which are now making in opinions and in institutions, may be claimed chiefly by men who have been indebted to his writings, and to the spirit of his philosophy, for the most important part of their intellectual cultivation.

I had originally proposed in this part of my work to give a slight sketch of the principal tenets of Bentham, with an exposition of what

I conceive to be his errors; pointing out at once the benefits he has conferred, and also the mischief he has effected. But slight as would be that sketch, it must necessarily be somewhat abstract; and I have therefore, for the sake of the general reader, added it to the volume in the form of an appendix.* I have there, regarding him as a legislator and a moralist, ventured to estimate him much more highly in the former capacity than the latter; endeavouring to combat the infallibility of his application of the principle of Utility, and to show the dangerous and debasing theories, which may be, and are, deduced from it. Even, however, in legislation, his greatest happiness principle is not so clear and undeniable as it is usually conceded to be. " The greatest happiness of the greatest number " is to be our invariable guide! Is it so? — the greatest happiness of the greatest number of men living, I suppose, not of men to come; for if of all posterity, what legislator can be our guide? who can prejudge the future? Of men living, then?— well—how often would *their* greatest happiness consist in concession to their greatest errors?

In the dark ages, (said once to me very hap-

* See Appendix B.

pily the wittiest writer of the day, and one who has perhaps done more to familiarize Bentham's general doctrines to the public than any other individual,) in the dark ages, it would have been for the greatest happiness of the greatest number to burn the witches; it must have made the greatest number, (all credulous of wizardry,) very uncomfortable to refuse their request for so reasonable a conflagration; they would have been given up to fear and disquietude — they would have imagined their safety disregarded and their cattle despised—if witches were to live with impunity, riding on broomsticks, and sailing in oyster-shells;—*their happiness* demanded a bonfire of old women. To grant such a bonfire would have been really to consult the greatest happiness of the greatest number, yet ought it to have been the principle of wise, nay, of perfect, (for so the dogma states,) of unimpugnable legislation? In fact, the greatest happiness principle, is an excellent general rule, but it is not an undeniable axiom.

We may observe, that whatever have been the workings of English philosophy in this age, they have assumed as their characteristic a *material* shape. No new, idealizing school has sprung up amongst us, to confute and combat with the successors of Locke; to counterbalance the attraction towards schools, dealing only with the unelevating practices of the world — the science of money-making, and the passionate warfare with social abuses. And this is the more remarkable, because, both in Scotland and in Germany, the light of the Material Schools has already waxed dim and faint, and Philosophy directs her gaze to more lofty stars, out of the reach of this earth's attraction.

But what is it that in Germany sustains the undying study of pure ethical philosophy? and what is it that in Scotland has kept alive the metaphysical researches so torpid here? It is the system of professorships and endowments. And, indeed, such a system is far more necessary in the loud and busy action of a free commercial people, than it is in the deep quiet of a German state. With us it is the sole means by which we shall be able to advance a science that *cannot* by any possible chance remunerate or maintain its poorer disciples in all its speculative dignity, preserved from sinking into the more physical or more material studies which to greater fame attach greater rewards. Professorships compel a constant demand for ethical research, while they afford a serene leisure for its supply ; insensibly they *create* the taste upon which they are *forced*, and maintain the moral glories of the nation abroad, while they contribute to rectify and to elevate its character at home.*

* Since writing the above, I have had great pleasure in reading a Petition from Glasgow, praying for endowed Lectureships in Mechanics' Institutes. I consider such a Petition more indicative of a profound and considerate spirit of liberalism than almost any other, which, for the last three years, has been presented to the Legislative Assembly.

# CHAPTER VII.

## PATRONAGE.

BEFORE touching upon the state of science,
and the state of art in England, it may be as
well to settle one point, important to just
views of either.  It is this —What is the real
influence of patronage?  Now, Sir, I hold that
this question has not been properly considered.
Some attribute every efficacy to patronage,
others refuse it all; to my judgment, two distinct sorts of patronage are commonly confounded: there is the patronage of individuals,
and there is the patronage of the State.  I con-

sider the patronage of individuals hurtful *whenever it is neither supported nor corrected by diffused knowledge among the public at large*—but that of the state is usually beneficial. In England, we have no want of patronage, in art at least, however common the complaint; we have abundant patronage, but it is all of one kind; it is individual patronage; the State patronizes nothing.

Now, Sir, I think that where the Public is supine, the patronage of individuals is injurious; first, because wherever, in such a case, there is individual patronage, must come the operation of individual taste. George the Fourth (for with us a king is as an individual, not as the state) admired the low Dutch school of painting, and Boors and candlesticks became universally the rage. In the second place, and this has never been enough insisted upon; the domestic habits of a nation exercise great influence upon its arts. If people do not live in large houses, they cannot ordinarily purchase large pictures. The English aristocracy, wealthy as they are, like to live in angular drawing-rooms thirty feet by twenty-eight, they have no vast halls and long-drawn galleries; if they buy large pictures, they have no place wherein to hang them. It is absurd to expect them to patronize the grand historical school, until we insist upon their living in grand historical houses. Commodiousness of size is therefore the first great requisite in a marketable picture. Hence, one very plain reason why the Historical School of painting does not flourish amongst us. Individuals are the patrons of painting, individuals buy pictures for private houses, as the State would buy them for public buildings. An artist painted an historical picture for a nobleman, who owned one of the few large houses in London; two years afterwards the nobleman asked him to exchange it for a little cabinet picture, half its value. "Your Lordship must have discovered some great faults in my great picture," said the piqued artist. "Not in the least," replied the nobleman very innocently, "but the fact is, *I have changed my house.*"

There was no longer any room for the historical picture, and the ornament in one house had become lumber in the other.

Individual patronage in England is not therefore at this time advantageous to high art: we hear artists crying out for patronage to support art; they have had patronage enough, and it has crippled and attenuated art as much as it possibly could do; add to this that individual patronage leads to jobbing; the

fashionable patron does every thing for the
fashionable artist.   And the job of the Royal
Academy at this day, claims the National
Gallery as a jobbing appendix to itself! —
Sir Martin Shee asks for patronage, and owns
in the same breath, that it would be the creature
of " interest or intrigue." But if it promote
jobbing among fashionable artists, individual
patronage is likely to pervert the genius of
great ones—it commands, it bows, it moulds its
protégé to whims and caprices ; it set Michael
Angelo to make roads, and employed Holbein
in designs for forks and salt-cellars.

No! individual patronage is not advantageous to
art, but there is a patronage which *is*—the patronage of the State, and this only to a certain extent.
Supposing there were in the mass of this country
a deep love and veneration for art or for science,
the State could do nothing more than attempt
to perpetuate those feelings; but if that love
and veneration do not exist, the State can probably assist to create or impel them.   The great
body of the people must be filled with the sentiments that produce science or art, in order to
make art and science become thoroughly naturalized among us.   The spirit of a state can form
those sentiments among its citizens.   This is the
sole beneficial patronage it can bestow.   How is

the favour of the people to be obtained? by suiting the public taste. If therefore you demand the public encouragement of the higher art and loftier science, you must accordingly train up the public taste. Can kings effect this—can individual patrons? They can at times, when the public taste has been long forming, and requires only developement or an impetus; not otherwise. It has been well observed, that Francis I, a true patron of art, preceded his time; he established patronage at the court, but could not diffuse a taste among the people; therefore his influence withered away, producing no national result; fostering foreigners, but not stimulating the native genius. But a succession of Francis the Firsts, that is, the perpetuating effect and disposition of a *State*, would probably have produced the result at last of directing the public mind towards an admiration of art; and that admiration would have created a discriminating taste which would have made the people *willing* to cultivate whatever of science or art should appear amongst them.

Art is the result of inquiry into the Beautiful, Science into that of the True. You must diffuse throughout a people the cultivation of Truth and the love of Beauty, before science and art will be generally understood.

This would be the natural tendency of a better
and loftier education—and education will thus
improve the influence of patronage, and probably act upon the disposition of the State.
But if what I have said of endowments be true,
viz. that men must be courted to knowledge—
that knowledge must be obtruded on them: it is
true also that Science should have its stimulants
and rewards.   I do not agree with Mr. Babbage,
that places in the Ministry would be the exact
rewards appropriate to men of science.   I
should be sorry to see our Newtons made Secre-
taries for Ireland, and our Herschels turned into
whippers-in of the Treasury.   I would rather
that honours should grow out of the natural
situation in which such men are placed, than
transplant them from that situation to one demanding far less exertion of genius in general,
and far less adapted in itself to the peculiar
genius they have displayed.   What I assert is
this,—that the State should not seem insensible
to the services and distinction of any class of
men—that it should have a lively sympathy
with the honour it receives from the triumphant
achievements either of art or science,—and that
if it grant reward to any other species of merit,
it should (not for the sake of distinguishing immortality, but for the sake of elevating public

opinion,) grant honours to those who have enforced the love of the beautiful, or the knowledge
of the true. I agree with certain economists—
that patronage alone cannot produce a great
artist or a great philosopher ; I agree with them
that it is only through a superficial knowledge
of history, that seeing at the same time an age
of patrons and an age of art and science, vain
enthusiasts have asserted that patronage produced the art ; I agree with them that Phidias
was celebrated through Greece *before* he was
honoured by Pericles ; I agree with them that
to make Sir Isaac Newton Master of the Mint
was by no means an advancement to Astro-
nomy ; I agree with them that no vulgar hope
of patronage can produce a great discovery or a
great picture ; that so poor and mercenary an
inspiration is not even present to the conceiving
thought of those majestic minds that are alone
endowed with the power of creation. But it is
not to produce a few great men, but to diffuse
throughout a whole country a respect and veneration for the purer distinctions of the human
mind, that I desire to see a State bestowing
honours upon the promoters of her science and
art; it is not for the sake of stimulating the lofty,
but refining the vulgar, mind, that we should
accustom ourselves to behold rank become the

natural consequence of triumphant intellect.  If it were the custom of this country to promote and honour art and science, I believe we should probably not create either a Newton or a Michael Angelo ; but we should by degrees imbue the public mind with a respect for the unworldly greatness which yet acquires worldly distinction (for it is the wont of the commercial spirit to regard most those qualities which enable the possessor to get on the most in the world) ; and we should diffuse throughout the community a respect for intellect, just as, if we honoured virtue, we should diffuse throughout a community a respect for virtue.  That Humboldt should be a Minister of State has not produced new Humboldts, but it has created throughout the circles around him (which in their turn act upon general society,) an attention to and culture of the science which Humboldt adorns.  The King of Bavaria is attached to art : he may not make great artists, but he circulates through his court a general knowledge of art itself.  I repeat, the true object of a State is less to produce a few elevated men, than to diffuse a respect for all principles that serve to elevate.  If it were possible, which in the present state of feeling must be merely a philosophical theory and suggestion, to confer peerages merely for life upon men of eminent intellectual distinction, it would gradually exalt the character of the peerage ; it would popularize it with the people, who would see in it a reward for all classes of intellect, and not for military, legal, and political adventurers only ; it would diminish, in some respect, the vulgar and exclusive veneration for mere birth and mere wealth, and though it would not stimulate the few self-dependent minds to follow art or science for itself, it would create among the mass, (which is a far more important principle of the two,) that general cultivation of art and science which we find is ever the consequence of affixing to any branch of human acquirement high worldly rewards.* The best part of the celebrated book of Helvetius is that which proves that the honours of a state direct the esteem of the people, and that according to the esteem of the people is the *general* direction

* "Oh," but say some, "these peerages would become the result of mere Court favour." I doubt it. Wherever talent forces itself into our aristocracy, not having wealth to support it, the talent, however prostituted, is usually the most eminent of its class. Whatever soldiers, whatever sailors, whatever lawyers, or whatever orators, climbing, not buying their way upward, ascend to the Hereditary Chamber, are usually the best soldiers, sailors, lawyers, and orators of the day. This would probably be yet more the case with men whose intellect dabbles less in the stirring interests of the world, and of whose merits Europe is the arbiter.

of mental energy and genius: " the same desire
of glory," says the philosopher, " which in the
early ages of the Republic produced such men as
Curtius and Decius, must have formed a Marius
and Octavius, when glory, as in the latter days
of the republic, was only connected with tyranny
and power; the love of esteem is a diminutive of
the love of glory;" the last actuates the few,
the first the multitude.   But whatever stimu-
lates in a nation the love of glory, acts also on
the love of esteem, and the honours granted to
the greater passion direct the motives of the
lesser one.

A Minister was asked why he did not promote merit : " Because," replied the statesman
drily, " merit did not promote *me !*"   It is ridiculous to expect honours for men of genius
in states where honours are showered upon the
men of accident;—men of accident indeed
amongst us especially,—for it is not to be high-
born alone that secures the dignified emolu-
ments of state,—but to be born in *a certain set.*
A gentleman without a shilling proposed the
other day to an heiress.   Her father delicately
asked his pretensions.

" I have little at present," said he, " but my
expectations are very great."

" Ah ! indeed—expectations !"

" Yes ;  you may easily conceive their extent, when I tell you that I have one **cousin a** Gren-ville and another a Grey."

To conclude, it seems, then, that the patron-age of wealthy individuals, (when the public is so far unenlightened that it receives a fashion without examining its merits) a patronage, which cannot confer honours,  but only confers money, is not advantageous to art or science,—that the patronage of the State is advantageous, not in creating great ornaments in either, but in pro-ducing a general taste and a public respect for their cultivation : For the minds of great men in a civilized age are superior to the influence of laws and customs ; they are not to be made by ribands and titles—their world is in them-selves, and the only openings in that world look out upon immortality.  But it is in the power of law and custom to bring those minds into more extensive operation—to give a wider and more ready sphere to their influence ;  not to create the orators, but to enlarge and still the assembly, and to conduct, as it were, through an invisible ether of popular esteem,  the sound of the diviner voices amidst a listening and reverent audience.

# CHAPTER VIII.

## THE STATE OF SCIENCE.

The public only reward in Science that which is addressed to their wants —The higher science cannot, therefore, be left to their encouragement— Examples of one man accomplishing the invention of another, often through want of mechanical means in the inventor—If the Public cannot reward the higher sciences, the State should—How encouraged here—Comparison between the Continent and England in this re. spect—Three classes of scientific men; the first nothing can discourage ; the last the public reward ; the intermediate class disheartened by indifference—Aristocratic influence deleterious by means of the Royal Society—Number of lesser Societies on *branches* of knowledge —The nature of Ambition—Its motives and objects common to philo. sophers as to other men.

I SHALL follow out through this chapter a principle advanced in the last.

Whatever is addressed to man's wants, man's wants will pay for ; hence the true wisdom of that doctrine in political economy which leaves the useful to be remunerated by the public.

Because, 1st. Those who consume the article are better judges of its merit than a Government.

2nd. The profit derived from the sale of the

commodity is proportioned to the number of persons who derive advantage from it. It is thus naturally remunerated according to its utility.

3rd. The inventor will have a much greater inducement to improve his invention, and adapt it to the taste or want of his customers than he would have were he rewarded by a Government which pays for the invention, but not for each subsequent improvement. Whatever, therefore, addresses the necessities of the people, the Government may safely trust to the public requital.

But it so happens that that part of science which addresses itself to immediate utility is not the highest. Science depends on some few great principles of a wide and general nature; from these arise secondary principles, the partial application of whose laws to the arts of life improves the factory and creates the machine. The secondary principles are therefore the parents of the Useful.

For the comprehension, the discovery, or the full establishment of the primary and general principles, are required habits of mind and modes of inquiry only obtained by long years of profound thought and abstract meditation. What the alchymist imagined of the great secret applies to all the arcana of nature. "The glorified spirit," "the mastery of masterships," are to be won but by that absorbed and devout attention of which the greater souls are alone capable ; and the mooned loveliness and divinity of Nature reveals itself only to the rapt dreamer upon lofty and remote places.

But minds of this class are rare—the principles to which they are applied are few. No national encouragement could perhaps greatly increase the number of such minds or of such principles.

There is a second class of intellect which applies itself to the discovery of less general principles.

There is a third class of intellect, which applies successfully principles already discovered to purposes of practical utility. For this last a moderate acquaintance with science, aided by a combining mind, and a knowledge of the details of the workshop, joined perhaps to a manual dexterity in mechanic or chemical arts, are, if essential, commonly sufficient.

The third class of intellect is rarely joined to the second, still more rarely to the first ; but *though the lowest, it is the only one that the public remunerate, and the only one therefore safely to be left to public encouragement.*

Supposing, too, a man discover some striking and most useful theory, the want of capital, or the imperfect state of the mechanical arts, may render it impossible for him to apply his invention to practical purposes. This is proved by the whole history of scientific discovery. I adduce a few examples.

The doctrine of latent heat, on which the great improvement of the steam-engine rested, was the discovery of a chemist, Dr. Black. Its successful application to the steam-engine required vast mechanical resources, and was reserved for the industry of Watt and the large capital of Mr. Boulton.

The principle of the hydrostatic paradox was known for two centuries before it was applied to the practical purposes of manufactures.

The press of Bramah, by which almost all the great pressures required in our arts are given, was suggested by that principle, but the imperfect state of the art of making machinery prevented its application until very recently.

The gas called chlorine was discovered by a Swedish chemist about the year 1770. In a few years another philosopher found out that it possessed the property of destroying infection, and it has since formed the basis of most of the substances employed for disinfecting. In later times another philosopher found out its property of whitening the fibre of linen and woollen goods, and it shortly became in the hands of practical men a new basis of the art of bleaching.

The fact that fluids will boil at a lower temperature in a vacuum than when exposed to the pressure of the air, has long been known, but the application of that principle to boiling sugar produced a fortune to its inventor.

It is needless to multiply similar instances; they are of frequent occurrence.

The application of science to useful purposes may then be left to the public for reward; not so the *discovery* of the theories on which the application is founded. Here, then, there should be something in the constitution of society or the state, which, by honouring science in its higher grades, shall produce a constant supply to its practical results in the lower. What encouragement of this nature is afforded to Englishmen? Let us consider.

In every wealthy community, a considerable number of persons will be found possessed of means sufficient to command the usual luxuries of their station in society, without the necessity of employing their time in the acquisition of wealth. Pleasures of various kinds will form the occupations of the greater part of this class, and it is obviously desirable to direct, as far as possible, that which constitutes the pleasures of one class to the advantage of all. Amongst the occupations of persons so situated, literature and science will occasionally find a place, and the stimulus of vanity or ambition will urge them to excel in the line they have chosen. The cultivators of the lighter elements of literature will soon find that a profit arises from the sale of their works, and the new stimulus will convert that which was taken up as an amusement into a more serious occupation. Those who pursue science will find in the demand for elementary books a similar source of profit, although to a far less extent. But it is evident that the highest walks both in literature and science can derive no stimulus from this source. In the mean time, the profits thus made will induce a few persons of another class to enter the field. These will consist of men possessing more moderate means, whose tastes are decidedly and strongly directed either to literature or to science, and who thus hope to make some small addition to their income. If any Institutions exist in the country, such as lectureships or professorships, or if there are any official situations, which are only bestowed on persons possessing literary or scien-

tific reputation, then there will naturally arise
a class of persons, whose education is directed
towards fitting them for such duties, and the
number of this class will depend in some measure on the number of those official situations,
and on the fairness with which they are filled
up.  If such appointments are numerous, and
if they lead to wealth or rank in society, then
literature or science, as the case may be, will
be considered as a profession.  In England,
the higher departments of science are pursued
by a few who possess independent fortune, by
a few more who hope to make a moderate
addition to an income itself but moderate,
arising from a small private fortune, and by
a few who occupy the very small number of
official situations, dedicated to the abstract
sciences; such are the chairs at our universities: but in England the cultivation of science
is not a profession.  In France, the institutions
of the country open a considerable field of
ambition to the cultivators of science; in
Prussia the range of employments is still
wider, and the policy of the state, as well as
the personal disposition of the sovereign, gives
additional effect to those institutions.  In both
those countries science is considered a profession; and in both, its most successful cultiva-

tors rarely fail to be rewarded with wealth and honours.

The contrast between England and the Continent is in one respect most singular. In our own country, we occasionally meet with persons in the station of private gentlemen, ardently pursuing science for its own sake, and sometimes even acquiring a European reputation, whilst scarcely a similar instance can be produced throughout the Continent.

As the annual income received by men of science in France has been questioned, I shall select the names of some of the most eminent, and give, from official documents, the places they hold, and the salaries attached to them. Alterations may have taken place, but about two years ago this list was correct.

M. Le Baron Cuvier, (Pair de France.)

| | Francs | £ |
|---|---|---|
| Conseiller d'état  .  .  . | 10,000 | 400 |
| Membre du Conseil Royal  . | 12,000 | 480 |
| Professeur de College de France  . | 5,000 | 200 |
| Professeur Jardin des Plantes, with a house  .  .  . | 5,000 | 200 |
| Secrétaire Perpétuel de l'Académie des Sciences  .  . | 6,000 | 240 |
| Directeur des Cultes Protestants  . | unknown | |
| | 38,000 | 1520 |

M. Le Baron Thenard,  (Pair de France )

|  | Francs | £ |
|---|---|---|
| Membre du Conseil Royal . . | 12,000 | 480 |
| Professeur à l'Ecole Polytechnique . | 5,000 | 200 |
| Doyen de la Faculté des Sciences . | 6,000 | 240 |
| Professeur au College de France . | 5,000 | 200 |
| Membre du Comité des Arts et Ma-<br>nufactures . . . | 2,400 | 96 |
| Membre de l'Institût . . | 1,500 | 60 |
|  | 31,900 | 1276 |

M. Gay Lussac,

|  | Francs | £ |
|---|---|---|
| Professeur à l'Ecole Polytechnique . | 5,000 | 200 |
| —— à la Faculté . . | 4,500 | 180 |
| —— au Tabacs . . | 3,000 | 120 |
| Membre du Comité des Arts et Ma-<br>nufactures . . . | 2,400 | 96 |
| —— du Conseil des Poudres et<br>Salpetres, with a house at the<br>Arsenal . . . | 4,000 | 160 |
| Essayeur à la Monnoie . . | 20,000 | 800 |
| Membre de l'Institût . . | 1,500 | 60 |
|  | 40,400 | 1616 |

M. Le Baron Poisson,

|  | Francs | £ |
|---|---|---|
| Membre du Conseil Royal . | 12,000 | 480 |
| Examinateur à l'Ecole Polytechnique | 6,000 | 240 |
| Membre du Bureau des Longitudes | 6,000 | 240 |
| Professeur de Mécanique à la Faculté |  |  |
| Membre de l'Institût . . | 1,500 | 60 |
|  | 25,500 | 1020 |

These are the fixed sources of income of
some of the most eminent men of science in

France; they receive some additions from being named as members of various temporary commissions, and it appears that these four persons were two years back paid annually 5432*l.* and that two of them had houses attached to their offices.

Without meaning to compare their merits with those of our countrymen, let us take four names well known in England for their discoveries in science, Professor Airey, Mr. Babbage, Sir David Brewster, and Sir John Herschel: without entering into detail, the amount of the salaries of all the official situations, which any of them hold, is 700*l.*—and a residence is attached to one of the offices!

Having thus contrasted the pecuniary encouragement given to science in the two countries, let us glance at the social position it enjoys in each.* The whole tone of public opinion in either country, is different upon the subject of science. In France, two of the persons

* The sordid and commercial spirit of our aristocracy may be remarked in the disposition of its honours. It is likely enough that there will soon be a numerous creation of Peers:—in France, such a creation would be rendered popular and respectable, by selecting the most distinguished men of the necessary politics;—*here,* neither the minister nor the public would ever dream of such a thing—we shall choose the *richest men !*

VOL. II.

alluded to were peers, and in the late law relative to the peerage, amongst the classes out of whom it must be recruited, members of the Institute, who are distinguished by their discoveries, are included. The legion of honour is also open to distinguished merit, in the sciences as well as in civil life; and the views of Napoleon in the institutions of that order are remarkable as coming from the military head of a nation, whose attachment to military glory is proverbial.

The following extracts from the speech of the First Cousul in 1802, to the Council of State, deserve attention:—

" La découverte de la poudre à canon eut aussi une influence prodigieuse sur le changement du système militaire et sur toutes les conséquences qu'il entraîna. Depuis cette révolution, qui est-ce qui a fait la force d'un général ? Ses qualités civiles, le coup-d'œil, le calcul, l'esprit, les connaissances administratives, l'éloquence, non pas celle du jurisconsulte, mais celle qui convient à la tête des armées, et enfin la connaissance des hommes : tout cela est civil. Ce n'est pas maintenant un homme de cinq pieds dix pouces qui fera de grandes choses. S'il suffisait pour être général d'avoir de la force et de la bravoure, chaque soldat pourrait prétendre au commandement. Le général qui fait de grandes

choses est celui qui réunit les qualités civiles.
C'est parce qu'il passe pour avoir le plus d'esprit,
que le soldat lui obéit et le respecte. Il faut
l'entendre raisonner au bivouac ; il estime plus
le général qui sait calculer, que celui qui a le
plus de bravoure. Ce n'est pas que le soldat
n'estime la bravoure, car il mépriserait le général qui n'en aurait pas. Mourad-Bey était
l'homme le plus fort et le plus adroit parmi les
Mamelucks ; sans cela il n'aurait pas été Bey.
Quand il me vit, il ne concevait pas comment je
pouvais commander à mes troupes ; il ne le
comprit que lorsqu'il connut notre système de
guerre. * * * Dans tous les pays, la force
cède aux qualités civiles. Les baïonnettes se
baissent devant le prêtre qui parle au nom du
Ciel, et devant l'homme qui en impose par sa
science. * * * Ce n'est pas comme général
que je gouverne, mais parce que la nation croit
que j'ai les qualités civiles propres au gouvernement ; si elle n'avait pas cette opinion, le
gouvernement ne se soutiendrait pas. Je savais
bien ce que je faisais, lorsque, général d'armée,
je prenais la qualité de *membre de l'Institut ;*
j'étais sûr d'être compris, même par le dernier
tambour.

" Le propre des militaires est de tout
vouloir despotiquement ; celui de l'homme civil

est de tout soumettre à la discussion, à la vérité,
à la raison.   Elles ont leurs prismes divers,  ils
sont  souvent  trompeurs :  cependant  la  discussion produit la lumière.   Si l'on distinguait les
hommes en militaires et en civils, on établirait
deux ordres, tandis qu'il n'y a qu'une nation.
Si l'on ne décernait des honneurs qu'aux militaires, cette préférence serait encore pire, car
dès-lors la nation ne serait plus rien."

It  is  needless  to  remark,  that  these opinions
are quite at variance with those which prevail in
England, and that military or political merit is
almost  the  only  kind  which  our  institutions recognize.

Neither then by station nor by wealth does the
practice  and  custom  of  the  State reward  the
English  student  of  the  higher  sciences;   the
comparison between England and the Continent
in this point is startling and decisive.   Two consequences  follow ;— the  one  is,  that  science is
the  most  cultivated  by  the  first  order  of  mind,
which  no  discouragement  can  check ;  and  by
the third order of intellect, which, applied merely
to useful purposes, or the  more  elementary and
popular knowledge,  is  rewarded  sufficiently by
the  necessities  of  the  Public ;  by that intermediate  class  of  intellect  which  pursues  the  discovery  of  the  lesser speculative principles, sci-

ence is the most disregarded. On men of this
class the influences of society have a natural
operation ; they do not follow a pursuit which
gives them neither a respected station, nor the
prospect of even a decent maintenance. The
second consequence is, that theoretical science
amongst us has great luminaries, but their light
is not generally diffused ; science is not higher
on the Continent than with us, but being more
honoured, it is more generally cultivated. Thus
when we hear some complaining of the decline of
science in England, others asserting its prosperity, we have only to keep these consequences in
view, in order to reconcile the apparent contra-
diction. We have great names in science : a
Babbage, an Herschel, a Brewster, an Airey,
prove that the highest walks of science are
not uncultured; the continuous improvement in
machinery adapted to the social arts, proves also
that practical and popular science is not dispro-
portioned to the wants of a great commercial
people. But it is nevertheless perfectly true,
that the circle of *speculative* science is narrow
and contracted ; and that useful applications of
science would be far *more* numerous, if theoretical speculators were more common. This deficiency we can repair, only (in my mind) by increasing the number and value of endowed pro-

fessorships, and by that vigilant respect from the honours of the State, which improves and elevates the tone of public opinion, makes science a profession, and allures to its rewards a more general ambition by attaching to them a more external dignity.

We may observe too, that the aristocratic influence in England has greatly adulterated the destined Reservoir of science, and the natural Fountain of its honorary distinctions—I speak of the Royal Society.  In order to make the Society "respectable"—it has been considered in the first place, necessary to pay no trifling subscription for admission.  " It should be observed," says Mr. Babbage, " that all members contribute equally, and that the sum now required is fifty pounds ; it used until lately to be ten pounds on entrance, and four pounds annually."  Now men of science have not yet found the philosopher's stone, and many whom the society ought most to seek for its members, would the most shrink from its expense.  In the second place, to make it " respectable" the aristocratic spirit ordains that we should crowd the society as full as possible with men of rank and property. Imagine seven hundred and fourteen fellows of the Royal Society! How can it possibly be an honour to a man of science to be

one of seven hundred and fourteen men;*
five-sixths of whom, too, have never contributed papers to the Transactions!—the number takes away emulation, the admittance
of rank and station indiscriminately, and
for themselves alone, lowers and vulgarises
the standard whereby merit is judged. Mr.
Davies Gilbert is a man at most of respectable
endowments, but he is of large fortune—the
Council declare him " *by far* the most fit person
for president." An agreeable compliment to the
great men in that society, to whom Mr. Gilbert
in science was as a child! But, perhaps you
may imagine it an honour to the country, that
so many men of rank are desirous of belonging
to a scientific society? Perhaps you may deem
it a proof that they cultivate science?—as well
might you say they cultivate fish-selling, because
by a similar courtesy they belong to the Fish-
mongers' Company; they know as much of science as of fishmongery : judge for yourself. In
1827, out of one hundred and nine members
*who had contributed to* the Transactions, there

* But the most remarkable thing, according to Mr. Babbage, is, that a candidate of moderate scientific distinction
is pretty sure of being blackballed, whilst a gentleman of
good fortune perfectly unknown, is sure to be accepted.
Thus is a society of science the mimic of a fashionable club !

were—how many peers, think you ?—there was
—ONE!

"A sun-beam that had gone astray !"

I have said that the more popular and more
useful sciences are encouraged amongst us, while
speculations in the higher and more abstruse are
confined only to the few whom, in all ages, no difficulties can discourage.  A proof of this is in the
number and flourishing state of societies which
are supported chiefly by the middle classes, and
which mere vanity could not suffice therefore
to create.   In the metropolis, even in provincial
towns, numerous societies for cultivating Botany,
Geology, Horticulture, &c. assemble together
those of similar tastes; and elementary tracts of
all sizes upon all sciences, are a part of fashionable literature.   But what I have said of letters
generally, is applicable yet more to science,—viz.
that encouragement to new, to lofty, and to
abstruse learning is more than ever necessary,
when the old learning becomes popularized and
diffused.

Ambition is of a more various nature than
the shallow suppose.  All biography tells us
that men of great powers will turn early from
one pursuit not encouraged, to other pursuits
that are.  It is impossible to calculate how
much Science may lose if to all its own obstacles

are added all social determents. Thus we find that the same daring inventor who has ennobled our age with the construction of the celebrated calculating machine,* after loudly avowing his

* One word upon this,—the most remarkable discovery of the time.

The object of the calculating machine is not to answer individual questions, but to produce multitudes of results following given laws. It differs remarkably from all former attempts of the kind in two points.

1. It proposes to construct mathematical tables by the *Method of Differences.*

2. It proposes to print on plates of copper the tables so computed.

It is not within my present plan to attempt even briefly any explanation of its mechanical principles, but the views which mechanism has thus opened respecting the future progress of mathematical science, are too striking to be passed over.

In this first attempt at substituting the untiring efforts of machinery, for some of the more simple, but laborious exertions of the human mind, the author proposed to make an engine which should tabulate any function whose sixth difference is constant. Regarding it merely in this light, it would have been a vast acquisition by giving to mathematical tables a degree of accuracy which might vainly have been sought by any other means; but in that small portion which has yet been put together, other powers are combined —tables can be computed by it, having no difference constant; and other tables have been produced by it, so complicated in their nature, that mathematical analysis must itself be improved before it can grasp their laws. The existence of the engine in its present state, gives just reason to expect that in its finished form, instead of tabulating dissatisfaction at the honours awarded to science, has proclaimed practically his discontent at those honours, by courting the votes of a metropolitan district.   Absolute monarchs have been wise in gratifying the ambition that is devoted to *peaceful* pursuits ; it diverts the aspirations of many working and brooding minds from more stirring courses, and steeps in the contented leisure of philosophy the faculties that might otherwise have devoted the same process of intrepid questioning and daring thought to the more dangerous career of action.

the *single* equation of differences, which its author proposed, it will tabulate large classes of that species comprised in the general form of *linear equations with constant co-efficients.*

The future steps of machinery of this nature are not so improbable, now that we see realised before us the anticipations of the past.   One extensive portion of mathematical analysis has already fallen within the control of wheels. Can it be esteemed visionary to suppose that the encreasing demands of civilized man, and the constantly improving nature of the tools he constructs, shall ultimately bring within his power the whole of that most refined instrument of human thought—the pure analysis ?

# CHAPTER IX.

## THE STATE OF THE ARTS.

Late rise of the Art of Painting in England— Commencement of Royal
Academy—Its infidelity to its objects—In two respects, however, it
has been serviceable—Pictorial art higher in this country, and more
generally cultivated, than in any other—But there is an absence of
sentiment in our Painters—The influence of the Material extends from
Philosophy to Art—True cause of the inspiring effect of Religion upon
Art.—Sculpture—Chantrey—Gibson.—Historical painting—Haydon,
&c.—Martin—His wonderful genius—New source of religious inspiration from which he draws—His early hardships.—Portrait painting—Its
general badness.—Fancy pictures—Wilkie characterized.—Landscape
painting—Turner.—Miscellaneous—E. Landseer—Water-colours—Engraving—Arts applied to Manufactures—The caprices of Fashion.—
Silk-working—Anecdote of Court patriotism.—Architecture—Introduction of the Greek school—Corrupted not corrected it—The unoriginal always the inappropriate in Architecture as in Poetry — We
must find the first principles in the first monuments—Not of other
nations but our own.—Summing up of the above remarks.

EVERY one knows that the Art of Painting
cannot be said to have taken root among us before the last century;—till then we believed
ourselves to be deficient in the necessary imagination. — *We* who had produced a Milton
and a Shakspeare! But the art commencing

with Thornhill, took a vigorous stride to perfection, and to popular cultivation, from the time of Hogarth; and, corrupted on the Continent during the eighteenth century, it found in that era its regeneration in England.

From 1734, the number of English artists increased with so great a rapidity, that in 1760 we far surpassed our contemporaries in Italy and France, both in the higher excellence of painting and the general cultivation of the art. The application of the fine arts to manufactures, popularized and domesticated them amongst us. And the delft ware manufactured by the celebrated Wedgewood, carried notions of grace and beauty to every village throughout the kingdom. Many of Flaxman's first designs were composed for Wedgewood; and, adapting his conceptions to the pure and exquisite shapes of Grecian art, he at once formed his own taste, and created that of the public. Never did Art present fairer promise in any land than when Reynolds presided over Portraiture, Barry ennobled the Historical School, and Flaxman breathed its old and lofty majesty into Sculpture. Just at that time the Royal Academy (subsequent to the Chartered Society of Artists) was established. I shall reiterate none of the just attacks which of late have been

made against that institution. It is sufficient to
state, that the Royal Academy was intended for
the encouragement of historical paintings—that
it is filled with landscapes and portraits ; that it
was intended to incorporate and to cheer on all
distinguished students—that it has excluded
and persecuted many of the greatest we possess,
and that at this moment, sixty-five years after
its establishment, our greatest living artists,
with scarcely any exceptions, have *not* been educated at an academy, intended of course *to* edu-
cate genius, even more than to support it afterwards !* With the assumption of a public
body, it has combined the exclusiveness of a
private clique. I do not however agree with
its assailants, that it has been very effectively
injurious to art ; on the contrary, I think that
in some respects art has been unconsciously assisted by it. In the first place, though it has

* Martin was a pupil of Musso. Flaxman studied with
his father, and at the Duke of Richmond's gallery. He studied, indeed, a short time at the Academy, where he was refused the gold medal. Chantrey learned carving at Sheffield ;
Gibson was a ship-carver at Liverpool. When Sir Tho-
mas Lawrence became a probationer for admission to the
schools of the Academy, his claims were not allowed. The
Academy taught not Bonnington—no—nor Danby, nor
Stanfield. Dr. Monro directed the taste of Turner.—See
an article in the New Monthly Magazine, on the Royal
Academy, May 1833.

not fostered genius, it has diffused through a large circle a respectable mediocrity, that is, it has made the standard of the Mediocre several degrees higher than it was before. And secondly, its jealousy and exclusiveness, though in some instances repressing the higher art they refused to acknowledge, have nerved it in others to new flights by the creative stimulus of indignation. For nobly has Haydon said, though, alas! the aphorism is not universally just, " Look down upon Genius and he will rise to a giant — attempt to crush him and he will soar to a god !"

The pictorial art is at this moment as high perhaps in this country as in any other, despite the rivalry of Munich and of Paris. I call to witness the names of Martin, Haydon, Wilkie, Landseer, Turner, Stanfield. It is also more generally cultivated and encouraged. Witness the number of artists and the general prices of pictures. It is rather a singular fact, that in no country abroad do you see many pictures in the houses of the gentry or lesser nobles. But with us they are a necessary part of furniture. A house-agent taking a friend of mine over a London house the other day, and praising it to the skies, concluded with, " And when, sir, the dining-room is completely furnished—handsome red curtains, sir—and twelve good 'furniture pictures'—it will be a perfect nonpareil." The pictures were as necessary as the red curtains.

But as in the connexion between literature, art, and science, whatever affects the one affects also the other, so the prevalent characteristic of the English school of painting at this moment is the MATERIAL. You see bold execution and glaring colours, but there is an absence of sentiment—nothing raises, elevates, touches, or addresses the soul, in the vast majority of our artists. I attribute this, indeed, mainly to the little sway that Religion in these days exercises over the imagination. It is perfectly clear that Religion must, in painting and in sculpture, inspire the most ideal conceptions; for the artist seeking to represent the images of Heaven, must necessarily raise himself beyond the earth. He is not painting a mere mortal—he cannot look only to physical forms—he must darken the chamber of his mind, and in meditation and fancy image forth something beyond the Visible and Diurnal. It is this which imparts the unutterable majesty to the Capitolian Jove, the voluptuous modesty to the Venus de' Medici, and breathes over the angry beauty of the Apollo, the mystery and the glory of the God. Equally in the Italian schools, the sentiment of Religion inspired and exalted the soul of the artist, and gave the solemn terror to Michael Angelo, and the dreamlike harmony to Raffaelle. In fact, it is not Religion alone that inspires the sentiment, but it is the habit of rousing the thought, of nurturing the imagination, which he who has to paint some being not " of earth earthy," is forced to create and to sustain. And this sentiment, thus formed by the severe tasking of the intellect, is peculiarly intellectual; and once acquired, accompanies the artist even to more common subjects. His imagination having caught a glory from the sphere which it has reached, retains and reflects it everywhere, even on its return to earth.* Thus, even in our time, the most striking and powerful painter we possess owes his inspiration to a deep and fervid sentiment of the Religious. And the dark and solemn shadow of the Hebrew God rests over the towers of Babylon, the valleys of Eden, and the awful desolation of the Universal Deluge.

If our houses are too small for the Historical School, they are yet still more unfitted for SCULPTURE: these two branches of art are

---

* Omnia profecto cum se à celestibus rebus referet ad humanas, excelsius magnificentiusque et dicet et sentiet.

CICERO.

necessarily the least generally encouraged. It is said, indeed, that sculpture is too cold for us,—it is just the reverse ; *we* are too cold for sculpture !

Among the sculptors of the present day, Chantrey and Gibson are pre-eminent : the first for portraits, the other for fancy subjects. The busts of Chantrey possess all those qualities that captivate the originals, and content their friends. He embellishes at once nature and art. If, however, the costume of his whole-length figures is in most cases appropriate and picturesque, (witness the statue of James Watt,) the statue of Pitt, in Hanover-square, is a remarkable exception, in which common-place drapery sits heavy on a disagreeable figure. It is much to be regretted that, since this eminent artist has been loaded with orders for portraits, the monuments that issue from his factory possess none of that simple beauty which distinguishes his early productions, — such as the Sleeping Children at Lichfield Cathedral, and the Lady L. Russell. The intention and execution of those performances raised him at once to a pitch of fame that *mere* portraits, however beautiful, cannot maintain. The highest meed of praise is, therefore, fast settling on Gibson, who now and then sends

to our Exhibition, from Rome, the most classical specimens of sculpture that modern times
have produced : they possess the grace—they
sometimes approach the grandeur—of the Past.
Next to the above, Gott and Campbell, at
Rome, and Westmacott, Baily, Behnes, Carew,
Nicholl, Lough, Pitts, and Rossi, in London,
possess considerable talent.

In hurrying over the catalogue of names that
have enriched the HISTORICAL department of
PAINTING, I can only indicate, not criticise.
The vehement action, the strength of colour,
and the individualising character of Haydon,
are well known.  Hilton, more successful in pictures of half-size life than the colossal, exhibits
in the former an unusual correctness of outline.
A certain delicacy, and a romance of mind, are
the characteristics of Westall.  But too great a
facility in composition, and a vagueness of execution, make us regret that very luck of the artist which, by too great a prosperity in youth,
forced and forestalled the fruits his natural genius, by slow and more painful culture, would
have produced.  Etty, practised in the colours
of the Venetian painters, if not strictly of the
Historical School, can be classed in no other.
His beauties are in a vigorous and fluent drawing, and bursts of brilliancy and light, amidst

an imitative affectation of the errors as well as excellence of the Venetian School.

But I hasten to Martin,—the greatest, the most lofty, the most permanent, the most original genius of his age. I see in him, as I have before said, the presence of a spirit which is not of the world—the divine intoxication of a great soul lapped in majestic and unearthly dreams. He has taken a range, if not wholly new, at least rarely traversed, in the vast air of religious contemplation; he has gone back into the drear Antique; he has made the *Old* Testament, with its stern traditionary grandeur— its solemn shadows and ancestral terrors — his own element and appanage. He has looked upon " the ebon throne of Eld," and imbued a mind destined to reproduce what it surveyed, with

> " A mighty darkness
> Filling the Seat of Power—as rays of gloom
> Dart round."

Vastness is his sphere—yet he has not lost or circumfused his genius in its space; he has chained, and wielded and measured it, at his will; he has transfused its character into narrow limits; he has compassed the Infinite itself with mathematical precision. He is not, it is true, a Raffaelle, delineating and varying

human passion, or arresting the sympathy of
passion itself in a profound and sacred calm;
he is not a Michael Angelo, the creator of gigantic and preternatural powers,—the Titans
of the ideal heaven. But he is more original,
more self-dependent than either: they perfected
the style of others; of Massaccio, of Signio-
relli;—*they* perfected others;—Martin has borrowed from none. Alone and guideless, he has
penetrated the remotest caverns of the past, and
gazed on the primæval shapes of the gone
world.

Look at his DELUGE—it is the most simple of
his works,—it is, perhaps, also the most awful.
Poussin had represented before him the dreary
waste of inundation; but not the inundation of
a world. With an imagination that pierces
from effects to the ghastly and sublime agency,
Martin gives, in the same picture, a possible
solution to the phenomenon he records, and in
the gloomy and perturbed heaven you see the
conjunction of the sun, the moon, and a comet!
I consider this the most magnificent alliance of
philosophy and art of which the history of
painting can boast. Look, again, at the Fall of
Nineveh; observe how the pencil seems dipped in
the various fountains of light itself: here the
moon, there the electric flash; here torch upon

torch, and there "the smouldering dreariment" of
the advancing conflagration ;—the crashing wall
—the rushing foe—the dismay of some, the resignation of others ;—in front, the pomp, the
life, the brilliant assemblage, the doomed and
devoted beauty gathered round the monarch,
in the proud exultation of his immortalising
death ! I stop not to touch upon the possible
faults, upon the disproportionate height of these
figures, or upon the theatrical effect of those ;
upon the want of some point of contrasting repose to augment the general animation, yet to
blend with it a softer sympathy ; or upon occasional errors in the drawing, so fiercely de-
nounced by rival jealousies ;—I speak of the
effect which the picture produces on all,—an
effect derived from the sublimest causes,—the
most august and authentic inspiration. They
tell us of the genius that the Royal Institution may form—it thrust this man from its
bosom : they tell us of the advantage to be
found in the patronizing smiles of aristocratic favour—let them ask the early history of
Martin ! If you would know the victorious
power of enthusiasm, regard the great artist
of his age immersed in difficulty, on the verge
of starvation, prying in the nooks and corners
of an old trunk for one remaining crust to

satisfy his hunger, returning with unsubdued
energy to his easel, and finding in his own
rapt meditations of heaven and heaven's ima-
ginings, every thing that could reconcile him to
earth !   Ask you why *he* is supported, and why
the lesser genii droop and whine for the patronage of Lords ?—it is because *they* have NO rapt
meditations !

I have heard that one of Martin's pictures
was undertaken when his pecuniary resources
could not bear him through the expenses of
the task.   One after one his coins diminished ;
at length he came to a single bright shilling,
which *from* its brightness he had, in that sort
of playfulness which belongs to genius, kept
to the last.   The shilling was unfaithful as it
was bright—it was taken with a sigh to the
baker's, declared to be a counterfeit, and the
loaf just grasped, plucked back from the hand
of the immortal artist.

In PORTRAIT-PAINTING—Lawrence, Owen,
and Jackson are gone ; the ablest of their successors (in oil) are Pickersgill and Philips: but it
may show the rottenness of individual patronage
to note, that while this department is far the
most encouraged, it has produced amongst us
far fewer painters of worth and eminence.   The
habit, perhaps, of painting so many vulgar

faces in white cravats, or velvet gowns, has toned down the minds of the artists to a correspondent vulgarity.

In FANCY-PAINTING we have the light grace and romantic fancy of Parris; the high-wrought elegance and chaste humour of Leslie (that Washington Irving of the easel); the pleasant wit of Webster; the elaborate yet easy charm of Newton. In Boxall, there is a tender and melancholy sentiment, which excels in the aspect of his women. Howard reminds us of Flaxman's compositions in a similar school—more the pity for Howard; and Clint, though employed in scenic representation, is dramatic —not theatrical. The most rising painter of this class, is Mr. Macclise: his last picture, " Mokanna raising the veil," is full of talent; but the face wants the sublimity of ugliness; it is grotesque, not terrible; it is the hideousness of an ape, not a demon.

But when touching on this department of the art, who does not feel the name of Wilkie rush to his most familiar thoughts? Who does not feel that the pathos and the humour of that most remarkable painter have left on him recollections as strong and enduring as the *chef-d'œuvres* of literature itself; and that every new picture of Wilkie—in Wilkie's own vein

—constitutes an era in enjoyment? More various, more extensive in his grasp than even Hogarth, his genius sweeps from the dignity of history to the verge of caricature itself. Humour is the prevalent trait of all minds capable of variety in character; from Shakspeare and Cervantes, to Goldsmith and Smollett. But of what shades and differences is not Humour capable? Now it loses itself in terror—now it broadens into laughter. What a distance from the Mephistopheles of Göthe to the Sir Roger de Coverley of Addison, or from Sir Roger de Coverley to Humphrey Clinker! What an illimitable space from the dark power of Hogarth to the graceful tenderness of Wilkie! And which can we say with certainty is the higher of the two? Can we place even the " Harlot's Progress" beyond the " Distraining for Rent," or the exquisite beauty of " Duncan Grey?" And if, indeed, upon mature and critical consideration, we must give at length the palm to the more profound, analytic, and epic grandeur of Hogarth's fearful humour, we have again to recollect that Wilkie reigns also in the graver domain to which Hogarth aspired only to record the limit of his genius. The Sigismunda of Hogarth, if not indeed so poor a performance as Lord Orford esteems it,

is at least immeasurably beneath the fame of
its wonderful artist. But who shall say that
" Knox," if also below the breadth and truth
of character which Wilkie carries into a more
familiar school, is not, for boldness of conception, and skill in composition, an effort of
which any master might be proud ? Wilkie
is the Goldsmith of painters, in the amiable
and pathetic humour, in the combination of
smiles and tears, of the familiar and the beautiful ; but he has a stronger hold, both over the
more secret sympathies and the springs of a
broader laughter, than Goldsmith himself. If
the Drama could obtain a Wilkie, we should
hear no more of its decline. He is the exact
illustration of the doctrine I have advanced—
of the power and dignity of the popular school,
in the hands of a master; dignified, for truth
never loses a certain majesty, even in her most
familiar shapes.

In LANDSCAPE-PAINTING, England stands
pre-eminent in the present age: for here no
academic dictation, no dogma of that criticism
which is born of plagiarism, the theft of a
theft, has warped the tendency of genius, or
interfered with the simple advice of Nature,
*whose face teaches.* Turner, Danby, and Martin, Stanfield, Copley Fielding, Dewint, Collins,

Lee, Callcott, John Wilson, Harding, and Stanley, are true pastoralists of the art. Turner was once without a rival; all that his fancy whispered, his skill executed. Of late, he has forsaken the beautiful and married the fantastic. His genius meant him for the Wordsworth of description, he has spoilt himself to the Cowley! he no longer sympathizes with Nature, he coquets with her. In Danby, a soft transparency of light and shade floating over his pictures accords well with a fancy almost Spenserian in its cast of poetical creation. In Stanfield, who does not acknowledge the precision of sight, the power of execution, the amazing scope and variety of design?

In MISCELLANEOUS PAINTINGS.—I pass over the names of Roberts, Prout, Mackensie, eminent for architectural drawings; of Lance and Derby, who almost rival the Dutch painters in the line of dead game, fruits, &c.; of Cooper, Hancock, Davis, distinguished in the line of Edwin Landseer, in order to come to Landseer himself. The extreme facility of this singular artist, renders his inferior works too sketchy, and of a texture not sufficiently characteristic; but in his best, we have little if any thing to desire. He reminds us of those metaphysicians, who have given animals a soul. He

breathes into the brute world a spiritual eloquence of expression beyond all literary power
to describe.    He is worth to the " Voice of Humanity," all the societies in England.  You cannot gaze on his pictures and ill-use an animal for
months afterwards.   He elevates your sympathies for them to the level of human interest.
He throws a poetry over the most unpoetical ;
nay, he has given a pathos even to " a widowed
duck ;" he is a sort of link to the genius of
Wilkie, carrying down the sentiment of humane
humour from man to man's great dependant
family, and binding all creation together in
one common sentiment of that affection whose
wisdom comprehends all things.   Wilkie and
Landseer are the great benevolists of painting : as
in the quaint sublimity of the Lexicon of Suidas,
Aristotle is termed " the Secretary of Nature,
who dipped his pen in intellect," so each of these
artists may be called, in his several line, the
Secretary also of Nature,  who dips his pencil in
sympathy : for both have more, in their genius,
of the philosophy of the heart than that of
the mind.

PAINTING IN WATER-COLOURS forms a
most distinguishing part of English art.  About
the end of the last century, a new style of
water-colour drawing or painting was adopted :

till then, whatever talent was observable in the
works of Sandby, Hearne, &c. there was no
particular difference in their method and the
works of foreign artists.  At the period above
mentioned, Dr. Monro, of the Adelphi,
an eminent amateur in that peculiar line,
invited several young men to study from the
drawings in his valuable collection, and under
his guidance : Turner, Girtin, Varley, and
others acquired a power of depicting nature in
transparent water-colours, that far outstrips
every thing previously produced.  Depth of
tone, without blackness; aërial distances, " the
glow of sunshine and the cool of shade,"
have been accomplished in a surprising degree,
not only by the three artists above mentioned,
but also by Glover, Fielding, Barret, Heaphy,
Richter, Stanfield, Cox, Holland, Harding, and
the German and wild and mystic pencil of
Cattermole.  But in many respects, the large
heads of expression, &c. by Sir Charles Bell are
the most extraordinary works in this department; and it is not a little remarkable, that,
in this style, a medical gentleman should have
pointed the goal to excellence, and an anatomist
have obtained it.

The art of ENGRAVING was in its infancy
among us a century ago ; in the course of a few

years, Strange, Woollett, Earlom, and Sharp carried it to its utmost vigour; but in our time, the application of machinery, and the system of division of labour, give to the practice perfection of line at the expense of sentiment and variety; the same means being applied on all occasions. This is observable in the Annuals and other works by the majority of our engravers. The sacrifice of the nobler qualities to mechanism reduces engraving to a trade; for the higher denomination of art can only be allowed where the unconstrained mind pervades the whole, keeping each part subordinate to and in character with the subject. John Landseer, Doo, the elder Engleheart, &c. &c. still, however, support engraving as an art. The like may be said of Reynolds the mezzotinto engraver. But this century may boast of having, in Bewick of Newcastle, brought wood-engraving to perfection; his pupil Harvey continues the profession with reputation.

One word on the ARTS applied to MANUFACTURES. There have for some time past been various complaints of a deficiency of artists capable of designing for our manufactures of porcelain, silk, and other articles of luxury in general use: we are told, that public schools are required to supply the want. It may be so, yet

Wedgewood, Rundell, and Hellicot the watch-maker, found no such difficulty, and now that a Royal Academy has existed sixty-five years, the complaint has become universal. One would imagine that the main capacity of such institutions was to create that decent and general mediocrity of talent, which appeals to trade and fashion for encouragement. In truth, the complaint is not just. How did Wedgewood manage without a public school for designers? In 1760, our porcelain wares could not stand competition with those of France. Necessity prompts, or, what is quite as good, allows, the exertions of genius. Wedgewood applied chemistry to the improvement of the material of his pottery, sought the most beautiful and convenient specimens of antiquity, and caused them to be imitated with scrupulous nicety; he *then had recourse to the greatest genius of the day, for designs and advice.* He was of course successful. But now the manufacturers of a far more costly material, without availing themselves of the example of Wedgewood, complain of want of talent in those whom they never sought, and whom they might as easily command, if they were as willing to reward. But the worst of fashion in its operation on art is its sudden caprices. China-painting was at its height about

1806.   Mr. Charles Muss, afterwards celebrated for his enamelling, was at that time a painter on porcelain: this application of colours was then a fashion, and ladies willingly gave him a guinea or more per lesson for his instructions. Within three years the taste subsided; ladies not only purchased less, but to a fashion for painting on china, had succeeded the fashion for painting on velvet.   Thence the fair students progressed to japanning, and at length settled with incredible ardour on the more feminine mysteries of shoe-making.

"With varying vanities from every part,
    They shift the moving toy-shop of the heart."

Trembling at his approaching fate, Muss by a vigorous effort turned from china to glass, (the art of painting on which was then little cultivated or understood,) but ere he could taste the fruits of his ingenuity, his family was in want of bread.   On a stormy night, drenched with rain, he anxiously pursued his way from Adam-street to Kensington, in the hope of borrowing a shilling.   His friend was in a nearly similar state of destitution; fortunately the latter, however, had still the blessed and English refuge of credit; and by this last remaining possession, he procured a loaf, with which the victim of these sudden reverses in feminine taste returned to his half-starved children.  But, alas!  the destinies of nations have their influence upon porcelain !   Peace triumphed on the Continent, and

" The tottering china shook without a wind !"

Compared with the foreign ground of China, that on which we paint is too coarse to allow equal beauty, whatever artist we employ : the fault is not with the painter, but in those who have not energy to ascertain and remedy the imperfection. They, it is true, have however the excuse, that in fashion every thing is novelty; to-day all must be ponderous and massive ornament ; to-morrow all must be fillagreed and minute.

A man whose service of plate is refashioned every ten years, will scarcely allow the silver-smith to expend the same price for designing and modelling, that was obtained when Rundell and Bridge, by employing the ablest designers in this country, supplanted competition. "Something handsome must be got up," and a meretricious and overloaded display is cheaper than exquisite execution ;  in some cases drawings have been sent abroad, to be there got up in metal at a cheaper rate.

With regard to silk-working: a few years ago a committee of gentlemen of rank and distinction, who took an active interest in the productions of British manufactures, obtained from France a sample of figured silk representing the departure of a young soldier; they felt confident that our own manufacturers could equal, or even surpass its excellence; but where could they procure a pattern with similar beauty and of national interest? They applied to a foreign gentleman in London, who immediately called on an English artist whom he considered adequate to the performance. The subject undertaken was a young sailor returned from a successful cruise: he hears that an old and valued friend is in prison for debt; he hastens to the gaol; he finds his friend tended by one, only visiter, (his young daughter,) in sickness and despair. The composition gave great and general satisfaction; but will it be believed that the idea of a British tar in a prison (even though visiting it for so noble a purpose) appeared to our sages in silk to be shockingly ominous? they therefore wished the back-ground to be changed into *a cottage!* The artist insisted very properly on the prison, and heard no more of the patronage of the committee. It is also an anecdote that for many years an aristocratic feeling prevented Wilkie's "Distraining for Rent" being engraved—*lest it should excite an unpleasant feeling towards the country gentlemen!*

In nothing, Sir, to my mind, is the material and unelevated character which belongs generally to the intellectual spirit of our times more developed than in our national ARCHITECTURE. A stranger in our streets is struck with the wealth, the gaud, the comfort, the bustle, the animation. But how rarely is he impressed with the vast and august simplicity, that is the result in architecture, as in letters, of a lofty taste, and the witness of a people penetrated with a passion for the *great!* The first thing that strikes us in England is the lowness of all the public buildings—they appear uncompleted; you would imagine a scythe had been drawn across them in the middle: they seem dedicated to St. Denis, after he had lost his head. The next thing that strikes you in them is the want of originality—they are odd, but unoriginal. Now, wherever an architecture is not original, it is sure to be inappropriate: we transplant what belongs to one climate to another wholly distinct from it—what is associated with one history or religion, to a site in which the history and religion are ludicrously opposed to it.

The celebrated Steuart, who sought to introduce amongst us the knowledge of the Grecian principles of architectural elegance, has in

reality corrupted rather than corrected taste.
Even he himself, laying down " The Appropriate," as a necessary foundation in the theory
of architecture, neglects it in his practice.
Look at yonder chapel, it is perfectly uncon-
nected and inharmonious with the character of
the building attached to it; assuredly it is the
most elegant chapel we can boast of—but you
would imagine it must be designed for the de-
votions of some fastidious literary institution, or
the " daintie oratoire" of a Queen.  No! it is
designed for our jolly tars, and the most refined
temple is dedicated to the rudest worshippers.
The followers of Steuart have made this want
of suiting the design to the purpose still more
ridiculous.  On a church dedicated to St. Philip
we behold the ox-heads typical of Jupiter; and
on the frieze of a building consecrated to a quiet
literary society, with whom prancing horses and
panting riders have certainly no connexion, we
see the bustling and fiery procession of a Grecian cavalcade.  The Greek architecture, even
in its purity, is not adapted to a gloomy and
chilling climate; all our associations connect it
with bright skies and " a garden life ;" but when
its grand proportions are omitted, and its minute details of alien and *unnaturalizable* mythology are carefully preserved, we cannot but

think that we have adopted one at least of the
ancient deities, and consecrated all our plagia-
rised blunders in stucco to—the Goddess of
Laughter !

Few, indeed, amidst the wilderness of houses
in which common sense wanders distracted, are
the exceptions of a better taste in imitation.
But the portico of St. Pancras and the London
University are beautiful copies from antient
temples, if nothing more, and it is impossible
not to point out to the favour of foreigners the
small Ionic chapel in North Audley Street, and
the entrance to Exeter Hall, in which last there
is even a lofty as well as an accurate taste.

But as a proof of the sudden progress which
art makes, when divorced from imitation, I instance to you our bridges : Waterloo and South-
wark bridges are both admirable in their way—
they are English; we may reasonably be proud
of them, for they are our own.

For my part I candidly confess, however
I may draw down on myself the languid contempt of the would-be amateurs of the port-
folio—that I think, in architecture as in poetry,
we should seek the germ of beauty in the
associations that belong to the peculiar people it
is addressed to. Every thing great in art must
be national. Wherever we are at a loss for

invention, let us not go back to the past of other countries, but the past of our own—not to imitate, not to renew, but to adapt, to improve ; to take the old spirit, but to direct it to new uses. If a great architectural genius were to arise among us, a genius that should combine the Beautiful with the Appropriate, satisfy the wants, suit the character, adapt itself to the life, and command, by an irresistible sympathy, the admiration, of the people, I am convinced that his inspiration would be derived from a profound study of *our own* national monuments of architecture from the Saxon to the Elizabethan. He should copy neither, but produce a school from both,—allied at once to our history, our poetry, our religion, and our climate. Nothing is so essentially patriotic as the arts ; they only permanently flourish amongst a people, when they spring from an indigenous soil.

From this slight and rapid survey of the state of the arts in England, we may observe, first, that there is no cause to complain of their decline ;—secondly, that as those efforts of art most adapted to private favour have succeeded far more amongst us than those adapted to the public purposes of a state ; so the absence of state encouragement, and the preponderance of individual patronage, have operated prejudicially on the grander schools.  Even (with a few distinguished exceptions) our finest historical paintings, such as those of Martin, are on a small scale of size, adapted more for the private house than the public hall.  And it is mostly on achievements which appeal not to great passions, or to pure intellect—but to the household and domestic interests—that our higher artists have lavished their genius.  We see Turner in landscape, and Landseer in animals, Stanfield in scenes, and Wilkie, whose sentiment is purer, loftier, and deeper than all, (save Martin's,) addressing himself, in the more popular of his paintings, to the most fire-side and familiar associations.  The rarer and more latent, the more intellectual and immaterial sources of interest, are not those to which English genius applies itself.  We may note also a curious coincidence between the Royal Academy for Art, and the Royal Academy for Science ; both ridiculous for their pretensions, but eminent for their inutility — the creatures of the worst social foibles of jealousy and exclusiveness — severe to genius, and uxorious to dotage upon the Mediocrity which has produced them so numerous a family.

But as I consider that the architecture of a nation is one of the most visible types of its prevalent character, so in that department all with us is comfortable and nothing vast. A sense of poetry is usually the best corrector and inspiration of prose—so a correspondent poetry in the national mind not only elevates the more graceful, but preserves also a noble and appropriate harmony in the more useful, arts. It is that POETRY OF MIND which every commercial people should be careful to preserve and to refresh.

# CHAPTER X.

## SUPPLEMENTARY CHARACTERS.

Lord Plume—Sneak—Mendlehon—St. Malo, the young Poet—His Opposite, Snap, the Philosopherling — Gloss Crimson, the Royal Academician.

LORD PLUME is one of those writers of the old school of whom so few are at present existing—writers who have a great notion of care in composition—who polish, who elaborate, who are hours over a sentence, which, after all, is, nine times out of ten, either a fallacy or a truism. He writes a stiff, upright hand, and values himself upon being a witty correspondent. He has established an unfortunate target in every court in Europe, at which he shoots a monthly despatch. He is deep read in memoirs, and has Grammont at his fingers'-ends: he swears by Horace Walpole, who would have made a capital butt of him. He reads the Latin poets, and styles himself F.R.S. He

asks you how you would translate ' *simplex
munditiis*' and ' *copia narium*'—takes out his
handkerchief while you consider the novel question, sighs, and owns the phrases are indeed
untranslatable.  He is full of anecdotes of the
by-gone scandal of our grandmothers : he
will give you the history of every crim.
con. which took place between a wig and a
farthingale.  He passes for a man of most
elegant mind — sets up for a Mæcenas, and
has a new portrait of himself painted every
year, out of a tender mindfulness, I suppose,
for the convenience of some future Grammont.  Lord Plume has dabbled greatly in
reviews — not a friend of his ever wrote a
book that he did not write *to* him a letter
of compliment, and *against* him an article of
satire: he thinks he has the Voltaire turn,
and can say a sharp thing or two.  He looks
out for every new book written by a friend
with the alacrity of a wit looking out for a
repartee.  Of late years, indeed, he has not,
however, written much in the Quarterlies,
for he was found out in a squib on his
uncle, and lost a legacy in consequence : besides, he is editing memoirs of his own ancestors.  Lord Plume thinks it elegant to
write, but low to confess it ;  the anony-

mous, therefore, has great charms for him : he throws off his jealousy and his wit at the same time, and bathes in the Castalian stream with as much secrecy as if he were one of its nymphs. He believes, indeed, that it would be too great a condescension in his genius to appear in the glare of day — it would create too great a sensation—he thinks men would stop each other in the street to exclaim, " Good God ! have you heard the news ? — Plume has turned author !" Delightedly, then, in his younger day, crept he, nameless and secret, into the literary world. He is suspected of having written politics as well as criticism, and retailed all the tattle of the court by way of enlightening the people. Plume is a great man.

From this gentle supporter of the anony-mous press, turn for one moment to gaze on the most dirty of its disgraces. Sneak " keeps a Sunday newspaper" as a reservoir for the filth of the week ; he lets out a *cabinet d'aisance* for any man who wishes to be de-livered of a lie. No trader of the kind can be more obliging or more ill-savoured : his soul stinks of his profession, and you spit when you hear his name. Sneak has run through all the circle of scoundrelism : whatever is most base, dastardly, and contemptible, Sneak has committed. Is a lie to be told of any man? Sneak tells it. Is a Countess to be slandered? Sneak slanders her. Is theft to be committed? Sneak writes to you — " Sir, I have received some anecdotes about you, which I would not publish for the world if you will give me ten pounds for them." Sneak would declare his own mother a drab, and his father a hangman, for sixpence-halfpenny. Sneak sets up for a sort of Beau Sneak — crawls behind the scenes, and chats with the candle-snuffer: when he gets drunk, Sneak forgets himself, and speaks to a gentleman; the gentleman knocks him down. No man has been so often kicked as Sneak—no man so often horsewhipped; his whole carcase is branded with the contumely of castigation :— methinks there is, nevertheless, another chastisement in reserve for him at the first convenient opportunity. It is a pity to beat one so often beaten — to break bones that have been so often broken; but why deny oneself a luxury at so trifling an expense? — it will be some honour to beat him worse than he has been beaten yet! Sneak is at heart the most miserable of men; he is poisoned by the stench of his own disgrace: he knows that every man loathes him ; he strives to buoy himself from " the graveolent abyss" of his infamy by grasping at some scamp of a lord. One lord, with one shred of character left to his back, promised to dine with him, and has been stark naked of character ever since. Sneak has stuck up a wooden box in a nursery garden between Richmond and London, exactly of that description of architecture you would suppose him to favour : it is for all the world like the temple which a Cit erects to the Roman Goddess of Sewers ; here " his soul still sits at squat." The little house stares you in the face, and reminds you at once of the nightman its owner. In vain would ingenuity dissociate the name of Sneak from the thought of the scavenger. This beautiful effect of the anonymous system I have thus honoured with mention, in order that posterity may learn to what degree of rottenness rascality can be corrupted.

Mendlehon is a man of remarkable talent, and of that biting wit which tempts the possessor into satire. Mendlehon set up a journal, the vein of which ran into personal abuse ; Mendlehon then went nowhere, and himself and his authorship were alike unknown : he became courted — he went into society, his journalism was discovered and avowed. Since

then the gossips say that the journal has grown
dull, for it runs no longer into scurrility.
When the anonymous was dropped, the writer
came under the eye of public opinion, and his
respectability forbids him to be abusive.

Of all melancholy and disappointed persons,
a young poet in this day is perhaps the most.
Observe that pale and discontented countenance,
that air at once shy and proud.   St. Malo is a
poet of considerable genius; he gives himself
altogether up to the Muse—he is consumed with
the desire of fame ;  the loud celebrity of Byron
yet rings in his ears :  he asketh himself, why he
should not be equally famous :  he has no pleasure in the social world : he feels himself not
sufficiently made of : he thinketh " by and by
they will run after my genius : " he is awkward
and gloomy ;  for he lives not in the present :  he
plunges into an imaginary future never to be
realized.   He goes into the world thinking the
world must admire him, and ask "Who is that
interesting young man ?"   He has no sympathy
with other men's amusements, unless they either
write poetry themselves or read *his* own : he
expects all men to have sympathy with *him ;*
his ear and taste were formed early in the
school of Byron ; he has now advanced to the
schools of Wordsworth and Shelley.   He imi-

tates the two last unconsciously, and then wonders why his books do not sell : if the original did not sell, why should the copy ? He never read philosophy, yet he affects to write metaphysics, and gives with considerable enthusiasm into the Unintelligible. Verse-writing is the serious occupation of his life ; he publishes his poems, and expects them in his heart to have an enormous sale. He cannot believe that the world has gone round ; that every time has its genius; that the genius of *this* time is wholly antipoetic. He throws away thought and energy, and indomitable perseverance, and the enviable faculty of concentrating ambition, upon a barren and unprofitable pursuit. His talents whisper him " success,"—their direction ensures him " disappointment." How many St. Malos have I known !—but half of them, poor fellows, have married their first cousins, gone into the church, and are now cultivating a flower-garden !

But who is this dry and austere young man, with sneer on lip and spectacles on nose? He is the opposite to the poet—he is Snap, the academical *philosopherling*. Sent up to Cambridge to learn theology, he has studied Locke, and become materialist. I blame him not for that ; doubtless he has a right to his opinion, but he

thinks nobody else has a right to any *other*
opinion than *his :* he says with a sneering smile,
" Oh, of course, Locke was too clever a man not
to know what his principles must lead to ; but
he did not dare to speak out for fear of the
bigots." You demur—he curls his lip at you—
he has no toleration for a believer ; he comprehends not the vast philosophy of faith ; he cannot get beyond Hume upon Miracles ; he looks
down if you utter the word " soul," and laughs
in his sleeve ; he is the most intolerant of men ;
he cannot think how you can possibly believe
what seems to him such evident nonsense.   He
carries his materialism into all his studies; he
is very fond of political economy, and applies its
principles to all things ;  he does not think that
government should interfere with education,
because it should not interfere about money.
He is incapable of seeing that men must be induced to be good, but that they require no inducement to get rich ; that a poor man will
strive for wealth, that an immoral man will *not*
strive for morality ; that an ignorant man will
*not* run after knowledge ;  that governments
should tempt to virtue, but human passions will
tend to wealth.  If our philosopherling enters the
House of Commons, he sets up for a *man of*
*business ;* he begs to be put upon the dullest

committees ; he would not lose an hour of
twaddle for the world ; he affects to despise
eloquence, but he never speaks without having
learnt every sentence by heart.   And oh ! such
sentences, and such delivery ! for the Snaps
have no enthusiasm !  It is the nature of the
material philosophy to forbid that beautiful
prodigality of heart ; he unites in his agreeable
style, the pomp of apathy with the solemnity
of dulness.   Nine times out of ten our philosopherling is the son of a merchant, his very pulse
seems to enter its account in the ledger-book.
Ah Plato ! Ah Milton ! did you mean the lute
of philosophy for hands like these !

" And how, Sir, do you like this engraving
of Martin's ?"   Go, my dear reader, put that
question to yon gentleman with the powdered
head—that gentleman is a Royal Academician.
I never met with an Academician who did not
seem to think you insulted him by an eulogy
on Martin.   Mr. Gloss Crimson is one of those
who measure all art by the Somerset-house
Exhibition.  He ekes out his talk from Sir
Joshua Reynolds's discourses—he is very fond
of insisting on the necessity of study and labour,
and of copying the antique.  " Sir," quoth
he, one day, " painting is the synonym of per-

severance." He likes not the company of young artists; he is angry if invited to meet them; he calls them indiscriminately " shallow coxcombs." He is a great worshipper of Dr. Johnson, and tells you that Dr. Johnson extolled the project of the Academy. Alas, he little knows that the good doctor somewhere wonders what people can be thinking of to talk of such trifles as an Academy for Painting! He is intensely jealous, and more exclusive than a second-rate Countess; he laments the decay of patronage in this country; he believes every thing in art depends upon lords; he bows to the ground when he sees an earl; and thinks of Pericles and Leo X. His colours are bright and gaudy as a Dutchman's flower-garden, for they are put on with an eye to the Exhibition, in which every thing goes by glare. He has a great notion of the dignity of portrait-painting. He would like to say to you, " Sir, I have painted four Earls this year, and a Marchioness, and if that's not a high school of painting, tell me what is!" He has a great contempt for Haydon, and is sure "the nobility won't employ him." He thinks the National Gallery a necessary perquisite of the Royal Academicians. " Lord, Sir," saith he, " if *we* did not manage the matter, there would be no discrimination, and you might see Mr. Howard's pictures in no better a situation than"—

" Mr. Martin's—that *would* be a shame !"

And so much, dear Sir, for characters that may serve to illustrate a few of the intellectual influences of the time.

# BOOK THE FIFTH.

---

# A VIEW OF OUR POLITICAL STATE.

### INSCRIBED TO

## THE ENGLISH PEOPLE.

" Since the affairs of men rest still uncertain,
Let's reason with the worst that may befall."

SHAKSPEARE.

" Si quid novisti rectius istis
Candidus imperti—si non, his utere mecum."

HORAT.

# CHAPTER I.

---

Address to the People.—Resumé of the principal bearings of former portions of this work.—Our social errors or abuses not attributable either to a Monarchy or an Established Church.

IF, my dear countrymen, you can spare a few minutes from the very great bustle in which you all seem to be at present; if you can cease for awhile from the agreeable duties of abusing the Ministry, reckoning up your bad debts, deploring the state of the markets, and wondering what is to become of you; if you can spare a few minutes to listen to your neighbour, who has your interest always at heart; he flatters himself that you will possibly find you have not entirely thrown away your time.

I inscribe to you this, my fifth book, which comprehends a survey of our political state, because, between you and me, I shrewdly suspect that the condition of the country is more your concern than that of any one else. Certain politicians, it is true, are of opinion that patriotism is an oligarchical virtue, and that the people are only anxious to go to the Devil as fast as they possibly can. To hear them, one must suppose that you are the greatest fools in existence, and that every piece of advice you are in the habit of giving to your rulers tends only to implore them to ruin you with all convenient dispatch. For my part, I do not believe these gentlemen; without thinking you either saints or sages, you have always seemed to me sensible persons, who have a very quick eye to your own interests, and seldom insist much upon any thing that, if granted, would operate greatly to your disadvantage. I inscribe this book to you, and we will now proceed to its contents.

I am obliged to suppose that you have read the preceding sections of the work—it is a bold hypothesis, I know, but we reasoners cannot get on without taking something for granted. Now, in all states, there is some one predominant influence, either monarchical or sacerdotal, or popular, or aristocratic. What is the influence which, throughout the previous sections of this work, I have traced and proved to be the dominating influence of England; colouring the national character, pervading every grade of our social system, ruling our education, governing our religion, operating on our literature, our philosophy, our sciences, our arts? You answer at once, that it is the ARISTOCRATIC. It is so. Now then observe, many of your (perhaps) inconsiderate friends insinuate the disadvantages of a Monarchy and the vices of an Established Church—*those* are the influences which they assert to be hostile to your welfare. You perceive by the examination into which we have entered, that this is not the fact; whatever be the faults in any part of our moral, social, or intellectual system, we have not traced the causes of those faults to the monarchical influences. I grant that, in some respects, (but those chiefly the effects of a clumsy machinery,) we have something to complain of in certain workings of the Established Church. Tithes are unpleasant messengers between our pastors and ourselves, but, as we are about to substitute for these a more agreeable agency, we will not talk any longer of the old grievance : in the true English spirit, when the offence is over, we will forget and forgive. The custom of Squirearchical patronage in the Church, of making the cure of souls a provision for younger sons, gives us, as I have attempted to prove, many inactive and ineffective pastors. But this, you will observe, is not the necessary consequence of an establishment itself, but of the

aristocratic influence which is brought to bear
on the establishment : just as those vast expenses, which we have managed to incur, have
not been the fault of the representative system,
but of the aristocracy by which the system has
been corrupted : the two instances are parallel.
In penetrating every corner of the island, in
colonizing every village with the agents of civilization, in founding schools, in enlightening
squires, in operating unconsciously on the moral
character and spiritual teaching of dissenters ;
in curbing to a certain limit the gloomy ex-
cesses of fanaticism—in all this you behold the
redeeming effects of an ecclesiastical establishment,—effects which are sufficient, let us acknowledge, to atone tenfold for all its abuses,
and which even the aristocratic deteriorations
have not been baneful enough to destroy.

It is not therefore, my friends, against a Monarchy or against an ecclesiastical establishment,
that it becomes us, as thinking and dispassionate
men, to direct the liberalism of the age.  No,
it is against a very peculiar and all-penetrative
organization of the aristocratic spirit !  This is
very important for us thoroughly to understand
and fully to acknowledge.  This is a first principle, to be firmly established if we do not desire to fight in the dark against imaginary

thieves while the real marauders are robbing us with impunity.

Between ourselves, I see a large portion of the aristocracy ready at any opportunity to throw the blame of their own misdeeds upon the king or the unfortunate bishops. Be on your guard against them !

# CHAPTER II.

The King has no interest counter to that of the People—Corruption lucrative only to the Aristocracy—The last scarcely less enemies to the King than to the People—The assertion, that to weaken the Aristocracy weakens the Crown, contradicted—The assertion, that an Aristocracy protects the People from the Crown, equally false — Antient dogmas inapplicable to modern times — The Art of Printing divides, with a mighty gulf, the two great periods of civilization—A Republic in this country would be an unrelieved Aristocracy—The feeling of the People is aristocratic—A certain Senator's boast—The destruction of Titles would not destroy the Aristocratic Power—The advantage of Monarchy.

In examining the national character and our various social system, we do not find the monarchical influence pernicious; I might venture to say more, — we shall generally find the monarch the most efficient check to the anti-popular interests. Look to our later history! Do you not remark that, in all popular measures, the King has taken part with yourselves? —has taken part with the people? The concurrence of two branches of the legislature— the executive and the representative—has com-

pelled the reluctant assent of the hereditary
chamber. What interest has a monarch in the
perpetuation of abuses ? He, unlike the aristocracy, has nothing to lose by concession to the
popular advantage. What interest has he in
the preservation of game laws and corn laws—
of corporations and monopolies, or of the vast
and complicated ramifications from which aristocratic nepotism raises a forest of corruption
out of a single banyan ?—An easy people makes
a powerful King, but a weak Noblesse. No,
my friends, no—a king has nothing to gain
by impoverishing his people; but every lord
has a mortgage to pay off, or a younger
son to provide for, and it is for the aristocracy,
not the king, that corruption is a lucrative
system. Compare, at this moment, that which
a prime minister " does for his family" with
that which his royal master can do for his
own. Heavens ! what a storm was raised when
the King's son obtained the appointment of
the Tower ! Was he not compelled to resign
that petty command—so great was the popular
clamour—so silent the ministerial eloquence ?
But, my Lord Grey ! what son—what brother
—what nephew—what cousin—what remote
and unconjectured relative in the Genesis of the
Greys has not fastened his limpet to the rock

of the national expenditure? Attack the propriety of these appointments, and what haughty rebukes from the Minister will you not receive! The tongue so mute for the King's son, rolls in thunder about the revered heads of the innumerable and unimpugnable Greyides. A king stands aloof and apart from the feuds and the jealousies—the sordid avarice—the place-hunting ambition—which belong to those only a little above the people. The aristocracy have been no less his enemies than ours—they have crippled his power while they have encroached on our resources. For the nature of that freedom which results from a privileged order partakes rather of the pride of arrogance than the passion for liberty.

"Ah, but," cry some, "if you weaken the aristocracy, you weaken the crown." Is that necessarily the case? Is a powerful aristocracy necessary to the safety of the throne? Look round the world, and see. Are not those monarchies the most powerful and the most settled in which the influence of the aristocracy is least strong, in which the people and the king form one state, and the aristocracy are the ornaments of the fabric, not the foundations? Look at Prussia, the best governed country in the world, and one in which the

happiness of the people reconciles us to despotism itself.  Believe me, my friends, where
a people are highly educated, absolute monarchy is more safe and less corrupting than
a grasping nobility.

Look again to the history of the states around
you ; so far from a king deriving strength from
an aristocracy, it is the vices of an aristocracy,
and not of a monarch, that usually destroy a
kingdom :  it is the nobles that take popularity
from a court—their scandal and their gossip
—their backstairs-creeping and gliding, their
ridicule of their master behind his back, their
adulation to his face — these are  the causes
that dim the lustre of royalty in man's eyes,
and vulgarize the divinity that should hedge
a king.  Impatient of the abuses of authority, the people do not examine nicely from
*what quarter of authority* the abuses proceed, and they concentrate on the most promi-
nent object the odium which belongs of right
to objects more subordinate and less seen.  I
say that an aristocracy, when corrupted, destroys, and does not preserve a monarchy, and I
point to France for an example :  had the French
aristocracy been less strong and less odious,
Louis XVI. would not have fallen a victim to
that fearful glamoury which conjured a scaffold

from a throne. That unfortunate king may justly be called a martyr;—he was a martyr to the vices of his *noblesse !*

I deny, then, the assertion of those who term it dangerous to weaken the aristocracy on the ground that by so doing we should weaken the monarchy. Henry VII. and Louis XI. may teach us wiser notions of the foundations of monarchical sway. I deny still more strongly that we require the undiminished power of the aristocracy as a check to the prerogative of the king. My good friends, you all know the old dogma, that a strong nobility prevents monarchical encroachment. Now, tell me candidly, do you not think we can take care of ourselves? Do we want these disinterested proxies to attend to our interests? For my part, I fear that we can but imperfectly afford such very expensive stewards. When we were minors in education, they might have been necessary evils; but now we are grown up, and can take care of our own concerns. Can you fancy, my dear friends, that if the aristocracy were not, " if it had bowed the head and broke the stalk, and fallen into the portion of weeds and worn-out faces,"* can you fancy that you would not

* Jeremy Taylor.

be equally vigilant against any very dangerous assumptions on the part of the monarch?
Trust me, while the looms of Manchester are
at work — while the forges of Sheffield ring
upon our ears—while morning and night the
PRESS unfolds her broad banner, visible from
John o' Groat's to the Land's-end, there is
but little fear that the stout heart of England should fall into so lethargic a slumber
that a king could gather armies without her
consent, construct dungeons without her knowledge, raise taxes without her connivance, and
wake her at last to behold a sudden tyranny,
and mourn for the departed vigilance of incor-
ruptible courtiers!

In truth, my friends, all those ancient arguments on the necessity of a strong aristocracy,
to check the king on the one side, and the
commons on the other, are utterly inapplicable now.  The checking power is not content
to be a check alone; it is like the sea, and
gains in every place where it does not recede:
as we have seen, it has entered, penetrated,
suffused every part of the very influences
which ought to have opposed it; and I tell
you once for all, my friends, that most of
the ancient maxims of polity dragged forth
from garbled extracts of half-read classics—

maxims of polity which were applicable to the world before the invention of printing, are for that very reason inapplicable now. Perfectly right, perhaps, were the statesmen of old in their scoffs and declamations against the people : the people were then uneducated, a mere brute physical force; but the magic of Guttenburg and Füst hath conjured a wide chasm between the past and the future history of mankind : the people of one side the gulf are not the people of the other; the physical force is no longer separated from the moral ; mind has by slow degrees crept into the mighty mass — the popular Cymon has received a soul ! In the primal and restless consciousness of the new spirit, Luther appealed to the people — the first, since Christ, who so adventured. From that moment all the codes of classic dogmatists were worthless—the expired leases to an estate just let to new tenants, and upon new conditions.

There is an era in civilization, when an aristocracy may be safely allowed a disproportionate strength, because an aristocracy is then composed of the best educated men ; and because their very haughtiness which fears liberty resists servitude.

In that era, men set apart from the baser

drudgeries of life, and devoted to the pursuit of arms, which in all times links itself with certain principles of honour, can scarcely fail of inspiring somewhat of refinement and of gallantry into the stubborn masses of an unenlightened society; their very ostentation promotes industry;—and industry, in diffusing wealth, expedites civilization.    But, as it is profoundly laid down by Montesquieu, " there is a very great difference between a system which *makes* a State great, and a system which *preserves* its greatness."    The era in which it is wise to promote a dominant aristocracy ceases when monarchs are not military chiefs, and the people of themselves can check whatever excess of power in the sovereign they may deem dangerous; it ceases when nobles become weak, but the spirit of aristocracy becomes strong; (two consequences, the result of a *numerous* peerage, which leaves half of the order mendicants upon corruption, but confirms the spirit which the order has engendered, by insensibly extending its influence throughout the subordinate grades with which it seeks intermarriage, and from which it receives its supplies; at that time chivalry has abandoned the nobles, and corruption has supplied its place;)—it ceases when an aristocracy is no longer in advance of the people, and a king and his subjects require no obstacle to their confidence in each other.

Thus then, neither for the safety of the king nor for that of the people, is it incumbent upon us to preserve undiminished, or rather uncorrected, the Aristocratic power.  But while both people and king can even do without an aristocracy, could you, my friends, do equally well without a king?  Come, let us suppose that the wish of certain politicians were gratified; let us suppose that a republic were established to-morrow? I will tell you what would be the result — Your republic would be the very worst of aristocracies!

Do not fancy, as some contend, that the aristocracy would fall if the king fell.  Not a whit of it.  You may sweep away the House of Lords if you like; you may destroy titles; you may make a bonfire of orb and ermine, and after all your pains, the aristocracy would be exactly as strong as ever.  For its power is not in a tapestried chamber, or in a crimson woolsack, or in ribbons and stars, in coronets and titles; its power, my friends, is in yourselves; its power is in the aristocratic spirit and sympathy which pervade you all.  In your own hearts, while you shout for popular measures, you have a reverential notion of the excellence of aristocratic agents; you think rich people alone "respectable;" you have a great idea of station; you consider a man is the better for being above his fellows, not in virtue and intellect, but in the good things of life. The most eminent of your representatives is accustomed to boast " that he owes his station to his father's industry in cotton-spinning:" you admire him when he does so—it is but a few weeks since that you rent the air when the boast was uttered; you fancied the boast was democratic and truth-loving. It was just the reverse—very aristocratic (though in a vulgar mode of aristocracy) and very false. Owes his station to cotton-spinning! Observe that the boast implies a pride of wealth, an aristocracy of feeling much more offensive than the pride of birth. Owes his station to cotton-spinning! If a man did so owe it, to my mind there is nothing to boast of, nothing very ennobling in the process of cotton-spinning. But what your Representative means to say, is this,—that the industry of his father in amassing an immense fortune is praise-worthy, and he is therefore proud of it; and you, my dear friends, being most of you employed in money-getting, are very apt to be charmed with the compliment. But successful industry in amassing money, is a very poor quality in the eyes of men who cherish high notions of morality; it is compatible with the meanest vices, with the paltriest exertions of intellect, with servility, with cunning, with avarice, with over-reaching! Compatible! nay, it is by those very qualities, that, nine times out of ten, a large fortune is made! They were doubtless not the failings of your Representative's father. I know nothing about that gentleman now no more; he enjoyed a high character; he may have had every virtue under the sun; I will willingly suppose that he had; but, let us stick to the point; it was only of one virtue that Sir Robert Peel boasted—namely, the virtue of making money. If this was an aristocratic boast, if it showed a poor comprehension of morality, so, on the other hand, it was not true in itself. And your Representative must have known it was not true while he uttered it. It is not true, that that distinguished man owes his station in the world to his father's industry; it is not true, that cotton-spinning has anything at all to do with it; he owes his station to his own talents, to his own eloquence, to his own perseverance—these are qualities to be proud of; and a great man might refer to them with a noble modesty; but *to please you*, my dear friends, the crafty orator only talks of the *to kalon* of cotton-spinning, and the *to prepon* of money-making.

Believe me then, that if you were to institute a republic to-morrow, it would be an aristocratic republic; and though it would be just as bad if it were an aristocracy of shopkeepers, as if it were an aristocracy of nobles, yet I believe on the whole it would be an aristocracy very much resembling the present one (*only without the control* which the king's prerogative at present affords him). And for one evident reason—namely, the *immense property* of our nobles and landed gentry! Recollect, that in this respect they differ from most other aristocracies, which are merely the shadows of a court and without substance in themselves. From most other aristocracies, sweep away the office and the title, and they themselves are *not;* but banish from court a Northumberland, a Lonsdale, a Cleveland, a Bedford, or a Yarborough; take away their dukedoms and their earldoms, their ribbons or their robes, and they are exactly as powerful, with those broad lands and those mighty rent-rolls, as they were before. In any republic you can devise, men with this property will be *uppermost;* they will be still your rulers, as long as you yourselves think that property is the legal heir to respect.

I always suppose, my friends, in the above remarks, that you would not *take away* the property, as is recommended by some of the unstamped newspapers, to which our Government will permit no reply, and which therefore enjoy a monopoly over the minds of the poor; I always imagine, that, republican or monarchical, you will still be English; I always imagine that, come what may, you will still be honest, and without honesty it is useless to talk of republics. Let possessions be insecure, and your republic would merge rapidly into a despotism. All history tells us, that the moment liberty invades property, the reign of arbitrary power is at hand;—the flock fly to a shepherd to protect them from wolves. Better one despot, than a reign of robbers.

If we owe so much of our faults and imperfections to the aristocratic influence, need I ask you if you would like an unrelieved aristocracy? If not, my friends, let us rally round the Throne.

# CHAPTER III.

---

BUT the Throne is expensive. Ah! hark to the popular cry :—

> " That's the wavering Commons ; for their love
> Lies in their purses, and whoso empties them
> By so much fills their hearts with deadly hate,
> Wherein the King stands generally condemn'd." *

The belief that the Throne costs something quite enormous is generally received in the manufacturing towns — thanks again to the unstamped publications, to which Lord Althorp, (desiring a republic, I suppose,) compels the poor — never will I be weary of urging the Government on that point !—And men, afraid to avow that republicanism is a good thing, delicately insinuate that it is an exceedingly cheap one. Let us see how far this is true ; let us

* Richard II.

subject our constitution to the multiplication table; let us count up, my friends, what a King costs us.

The whole of our yearly expenditure, including our National Debt, is somewhat more than fifty millions; out of this vast sum you may reckon that a King costs as follows :—

| | |
|---|---:|
| Civil list . . . . | 411,800 |
| Three regiments of Horse Guards | 80,000 |
| Pensions to Royal Family . | 220,000 |
| For servants to different branches of the Royal Family . . | 24,000 |
| | £735,800 |

These are the main expenses of royalty; I cannot find, by any ingenuity, that we can attach to it a much larger sum ;—but let us be liberal and reckon the whole at a million. What then? Why the King would only cost us just one fiftieth part of our yearly outgoings, or one twenty-eighth part of our National Debt!

I think, indeed, the royal expenditure might be somewhat lessened without diminishing the royal dignity. I see not why we should have three regiments of Horse Guards; but let this pass. Suppose we do not cut down a shilling of the King's expenses, is it not idle to talk of the oppressive cost of a King when it amounts only to a fiftieth part of our yearly incumbrances?

Ah, say some, but supposing the King were not, we should be better able to cut down the other expenses. I fancy they are very much mistaken; those expenses are the expenses that have no connexion with Monarchy — expenses that are solely for the convenience of the aristocracy.

Do you find that the King himself resists retrenchment? on the contrary, was not retrenchment the very principle established between himself and his ministers? Republics, I allow, are generally cheap: but then Republics have not generally run into debt as you have. I suppose, by being Republicans, we should not get whitewashed, and that we should be equally obliged to discharge our pecuniary obligations. But how was that debt incurred? My dear friends, that is quite another question; I am not arguing whether you might not be richer had you established a Republic a century ago, (though I doubt it exceedingly, for I could prove your aristocracy, more than your monarch, to blame for your debt,) but whether you would be much richer *now* by establishing a Republic? It is cheaper to build a plain house than a fine one; but having once built your fine house, it is a false economy to take it down for the purpose of building a plain one.

Some one pulls me by the arm and asks me, why I defend a Monarchy which the Whigs assure us that nobody attacks. Hark you, my good friends, the reason is this — I see much farther than the Whigs do, and I speak more conscientiously,—I hate the policy that looks not beyond the nose of the occasion. I love to look far and to speak boldly. I have no place to gain, no opinion to disguise—nothing stands between me and the Truth. I put it to you all, whether, viewing the temper of the age, the discontent of the multitude, the example of foreign states, the restlessness of France, the magnificent affluence of North America, the progress of an unthinking liberalism, the hatred against ostensible power— I put it to you all whether, unless some great and dexterous statesman arise, or unless some false notions are removed, some true principles are explained, you do not perceive slowly sweeping over the troubled mirror of the Time the giant shadow of the coming Republic?

# CHAPTER IV.

---

The House of Lords not to be confounded with the Aristocracy — Caution against the advice of journalists — Objections to a numerous creation of Peers — The people proved to be less strong than they imagine—The abolition of the House of Lords proved to be dangerous to the safe working of the Commons—A third mode of reforming a second chamber, but the people are not prepared for it.

BUT since it seems that our jealousy must be directed mainly against the aristocratic power, how shall we proceed in order to resist and diminish it ? That is a question not easily answered. Do not, my friends, do not let us confound a House of Lords, which is but a part of the aristocracy, with the aristocracy itself : there is just as much aristocracy in the House of Commons as there is in the House of Lords, only at this moment you are very justly displeased with the Lords. If you were to destroy that assembly, it would not be long before you would be quite as much displeased with the House of Commons !

Could I persuade you to take my advice,

you would look with considerable suspicion on the leading articles of newspapers ; especially when their writers seem very earnestly to take your view of the question. You know it is a common trick among thieves, when they see a green-horn engaged in a broil, to affect to be all on his side ; so in Roderick Random, an honest fellow offers very good-naturedly to hold Strap's coat for him while Strap enjoys a comfortable round or two at reciprocal fisticuffs. When the battle is done, Strap's coat has disappeared ! My dear friends, there are certain journalists who seem passionately in your favour —all willing to pat you on the back, and give you a knee, while you show your manhood on the House of Lords ! but recollect poor Strap, and keep your coats on your shoulders. This is the homely advice of your friend and neighbour.

Yes ! I see certain journalists strongly recommending a numerous creation of peers. Somehow or other, those journalists are very fond of the ministers : it is true they scold them now and then in a conjugal way ; but they make it upon a pinch, because, like man and wife, the journalist and minister often have an interest in common. There was a time when I advocated a numerous creation of peers—a creation that should bring the two Houses of Parliament into tolerable concord ; but that time is past. New objections have arisen to such a policy, and I confess that on my mind those objections have considerable weight. Are you willing, my compatriots, to give the Whig ministers such a majority in both houses, that you will never be able without revolution to have any other administration ? If so, then go on, clap your hands, and cry out with the Morning Chronicle for new peers ! Do not fancy that measures would be more liberal if this creation were made ! it is a delusion ! What would be this creation ? it would be a *Whig creation !* Ah ! I see that, sooner than such a creation, you would consent to have chaos a little longer ! You are right. Measures would not be more liberal ; on the contrary, it is from the despair of pleasing the Lords that the only really liberal measure of the Whigs (the Reform Bill) was insisted upon ! Do you not observe, the moment the two Houses may be brought pretty nearly to the same temper, that the Whigs are willing to pare down and smooth away any popular proposition, so that it may glide quietly from one House through the other ? If there were but little difference between the two chambers, depend upon it, in that little difference the people would invariably go to the wall.  Do you not mark, that as the ministers now cannot govern by the House of Lords, so they *must* govern somewhat by the people?  But suppose they had secured the House of Lords, the people would not be half so necessary to them.  It is the very opposition of the Tory aristocracy that has compelled the Whigs to be liberal.  Let them break that opposition entirely, and you will see the Whigs themselves rapidly hardening and encrusting into Tories.  There was a time, I say, when I thought a creation of peers desirable; but at that time I imagined we might safely trust the Whigs with so enormous a power.  I think otherwise now.  Give them the command of both the chambers, and you reduce the King to a cipher.  You make a Whig aristocracy perpetual.  "Oh!" cry some of the mob-orators, or our friends the journalists, "the people have now the power to get good government, and they will use it, let there be what ministry there may!"  No such thing, my dear friends, no such thing; we have *not* that power.  You have chosen your House of Commons, it is true, and a pretty set of gentlemen you have chosen!  "You talk," said one of the most enlightened of the ministers to a friend of mine,

" you talk of our fear of a collision with the Lords, if we should be very popular in our measures. Faith, in that case we should be equally afraid of a collision with the Commons. Look at the scatterlings of the Mountain Bench ; run your eye over Mr. Hume's divisions ; count the number of Radicals in Parliament, and confess that we have *not* a House of Commons prepared to receive with joy any *very* popular propositions." Was not the minister right ? Where, O English people ! where are your friends —where your supporters—where those securers of good government that the coat-holders talk of ! Yon few violent theorists, all quarrelling with each other, full of crotchets and paper-money chimeras ;—are *those* your friends ? The tenants of yon ministerial benches, to whom, were it not for yells and groans which savour but little of humanity, one might apply the line once applied to the stoics—

" Rarus sermo in illis, et magna libido tacendi,"—

are *they* your friends ? " No," you say ; " but if we had a dissolution !" Ah, *but in the mean while?*—the next five years ? Are we to throw *those* years away by granting Whig measures a certain monopoly of the whole legislature ? I think the experiment would be unwise in us;

But between ourselves, I fear. greatly that if Parliament were dissolved next week, though you would return many more Tories, and a few more independent members, you would still, under the present Reform Bill, return a sufficient majority of Whigs. The basis of the Reform Bill is property ; your own minds incline to the representation of property ; the Whigs possess the great proportion of that sort of property which is brought to bear in elections; their property will return them. So that were you to swamp the Lords, and then to proceed to a new election, you would still perpetuate the Whig dynasty. It is true that you might pledge your representatives; but I think you have seen enough of pledges. Do you know an excellent pair of caricatures called " Before and After ?" In the first caricature the lover is all ardour, in the second he is all frigidity. For a lover read a member—members' pledges are like lovers' oaths — possession destroys their value !

I beseech you, then, to pause well and long before you swell the cry for new peers, or before you are cajoled into believing that to strengthen a Whig ministry is the best mode of weakening an aristocratic domination.

A second mode of dealing with the House of

Lords has occurred to some bolder speculators—
they propose not to swamp it, but to wash it
away altogether.  Mighty well!  What would
be the consequence?  Why, you would have all
the Lords taking their seats in the House of
Commons.  You would have no popular assembly at all; you would transfer the Wellingtons,
and the Winchelseas, and the Northumberlands,
and the Exeters, and the Newcastles, to the
Lower House, as the representatives of yourselves.  Their immense property would easily
secure their return, to the exclusion of poorer
but more popular men, for the divided counties
in which it is situated; and all you would effect by destroying the existence of one chamber,
would be a creation of a Tory majority in the
other.

It was this which the sagacious mind of the
Duke of Wellington foresaw, when he declared
—as he is reported to have done in private—
that he would rather the House of Lords were
destroyed than swamped; and that in the former case he should be more powerful as Mr.
Wellesley, than in the latter as the Duke of
Wellington.

Trust me then, neither of these modes of
treating the Lords will be found to our advantage: a third mode might be devised — but I

think we are not yet prepared for it, viz. —the
creation of an elective, not an hereditary senate,
which might be an aristocracy in the true sense
of the word—that is, an assembly of the best
men—the selected of the country—selected
from the honest as the rich, the intelligent as
the ignorant—in which property would cease to
be the necessary title, and virtue and knowledge might advance claims equally allowed.
But I say no more on this point. For nothing
could give rise or dignity to such an assembly,
but that enlightened opinion among ourselves
which legislation alone cannot effect !

# CHAPTER V.

A Reformed Code of Opinion the best method of reforming the great Errors of the Legislation.

IT appears then, upon the whole, that the only safe, practical, and uncharlatanic resistance you can offer to the influences which are so pernicious, is in a thorough understanding of the extent and nature of those influences—in a perpetual and consistent jealousy of their increase—in wise, unceasing, but gradual measures for their diminution. You have observed that the worst part of these influences is in a *moral* influence. This you can counteract by a *new* moral standard of opinion—once accustom yourselves to think that

> " Rank is but the guinea stamp,
>   The mon's the gowd for a' that;"

once learn to detach respectability from acres and rent-rolls—once learn indifference for fashion and fine people; for the ' whereabouts' of lords and ladies; for the orations of men boasting of the virtue of making money; once learn to prize at their full worth—a high integrity, and a lofty intellect—once find yourselves running to gaze, not on foreign Princes and Lord Mayors' coaches, but on those who elevate, benefit, and instruct you, and you will behold a new influence pushing its leaves and blossoms from amidst the dead corruption of the old. To counteract a bad moral influence, never let us omit to repeat that you must create a good moral influence. Reformed opinion precedes reformed legislation. Now is the day for writers and advisers; *they* prepare the path for true lawgivers; they are the pioneers of good; no reform is final, save the reform of mind. Hence it is that I have written this book, instead of devoting the same time, like our philosopherling Mr. Snap, to the compilation of a score or two of speeches. The speeches would perish in a week; but the subject of this book must make it live, till its end be fulfilled. Others, with greater effect, because with higher genius, will follow in my track—" Je serais le mouche du coche qui se passera bien de mon bourdonnement. Il va, mes chers amis—et ne cesse d'aller. Si sa marche nous parait lente, c'est que nous vivons un instant. Mais que de chemin il a fait depuis cinq ou six siecles! A cette heure, en pleine roulant, rien ne le peut plus arrêter." *

* Pamphlet des Pamphlets.

# CHAPTER VI.

## THE STATE OF PARTIES.

The Tories; they are not extinct—Two great Divisions among them—
Sir Robert Peel described—His very Merits displease one Division
of this Party—That Division characterized—The Ultra Radicals—
—The Ministerial Party—Unity necessary to Government—The advantage of a new National Party.

HAVING defined, through the mists of
political delusion, the outline of the hostile
and the friendly encampments—having ascertained what powers we shall attack and what
defend, let us approach somewhat closer to
the actual field, and examine the state of those
contending parties, who, not sharing our views,
nor actuated by our motives, fight without
knowing wherefore or for what end, save, perhaps, that to the vulgar mass of the soldiery
there is some guiding and consolatory recollection that plunder is the perquisite of conquest.

THE STATE OF PARTIES: it is an interesting survey, and you, my dear friends, ought
to think it peculiarly interesting; for, as for-

merly men burnt each other out of pure affection for God, so now they all attack each other
like furies for no other motive in the world
but a disinterested attachment to the People.
Heaven grant that you may be better served
by *your* fanatics than our good Maker has been
by his !

Don't believe the coat-holders, my friends,
when they tell you with so assured an air
that the Tories, as a party, are extinct. They
are *not* extinct ; the spirit of Toryism never
dies. " You may kill men," said a French
friend* of your's once, and the saying is full of
the pith of that wit which is another word for
truth, " you may kill men, but you cannot kill
things." The Tories in a year or two hence will
perhaps be as formidable as ever. It is true
that Wetherell may wander seatless ; it is true
that Croker's sarcastic lip may no longer lavish
compliments on the treasury benches ; it is
true that Gatton is a ghost, and Old Sarum
a tradition ; but, my dear friends, till the future itself is no more, the past will have its
bigoted defenders, and the world will be in no
want of a Wetherell. And what though Gatton be defunct ? Trust me, the corruption of
a Norwich will engender the same fungus, that

* Volney.

sprouted forth from the rottenness of Gatton. But the Tories, even as a body of men so known and termed, are not extinct ; they have a majority in the Lords, and in the Commons they are at least three times as numerous as the ultra Radicals. Take the Tories at the lowest, there are a hundred and fifty of them in your own assembly : take the ultra Radicals at the highest, and you cannot number above fifty. Better, therefore, might you say, that the Radicals were extinct, than that the Tories were extinct. The last, I grant you, seem lethargic enough at present ; but, like the hare, they sleep with their eyes open, and, like the snake, they are hoarding venom.

But the main feature of all parties at this moment is, that in every party there are divisions. The Tories are weakened by bitter though unacknowledged schisms among themselves : in the Commons they fall into two main bands, the one following Sir Robert Peel, the other regarding him with suspicion, and half disposed to revolt from his side. " The following" of Sir Robert Peel are composed of men of a certain semi-enlightenment, of moderate passions, and a regard for peace above all things : they would rather retain the ministers than discard them ; they have no

desire for perilous experiments of Tory rule;
they have a horror of revolution, and possess
more of the timorous prudence of merchants
than the haughty courage of aristocrats. Whatever is Tory among the " more respectable" of
the metropolitan population — the bankers, the
traders, the men who deem it a virtue in their
fathers to make money by cotton-spinning—
all these are with Sir Robert Peel: they ex-
tol his discretion and confide in his judgment:
And, in truth, Sir Robert Peel is a remarkable man—confessedly a *puissance* in himself,
confessedly the leading member of the representative, yes, even of your reformed, assembly: he is worth our stopping in our progress for a moment in order to criticize his
merits.

It is a current mistake in the provinces
to suppose that Sir Robert Peel is rather
sensible than eloquent. If to persuade, to
bias, to soothe, to command the feelings, the
taste, the opinions of an audience, often dia-
metrically opposed to his views—if *this* be eloquence, which I, a plain man, take it to be,
then Sir Robert Peel is among the most eloquent of men. I am not one of those who
think highly of the art of oratory; I laugh
at the judgment of such as rank its suc-

cessful cultivation among the great efforts of mind : it depends mainly upon physical advantages and a combination of theatrical tricks ; a man may therefore have but ordinary intellectual powers, and yet be exceedingly eloquent to a popular assembly ; nay, we need only analyse calmly the speeches which have delighted an audience, to be aware of their ordinary lack of all eminently intellectual qualifications. That sentence which reads to you so tame, was made emphatic by the most dexterous pronunciation—that sarcasm which seems to you so poor, took all its venom from the most significant smile—that fallacy which strikes you as so palpable, seemed candour itself by the open air of sincerity with which it was delivered. Pronunciation, smile, air ! They are excellent qualities in an orator, but may they not be achieved without any wondrous depth of the reason, or any prodigious sublimity of the imagination ? I am speaking, therefore, in admiration of Sir Robert Peel's eloquence, and not of his mind ; though even in the latter he excels the capacity of orators in general.

Physical advantages are one component of successful oratory ; these Sir Robert Peel possesses—a most musical voice—a tall and stately person—a natural happiness of delivery, which

though not wholly void of some displeasing pe
culiarities, is more than ordinarily commanding
and impressive. A combination of theatrical
tricks is another component of successful oratory, and this also Sir Robert Peel has most
dexterously acquired; by a wave of the hand,
by a bow across the table, by an expression of
lip, by a frankness of mien, he can give force,
energy, wit, or nobility—to nothings! Oratory
is an art — he is an elaborate artist. In the
higher qualities of mind, he must be considered
a man of remarkable accomplishments. With
a wide range of ornamental, he combines a vast
hoard of practical, knowledge; he is equally
successful in a speech on the broadest principle,
or on the narrowest detail. He has equally the
information of a man of letters, and of a man of
business. He is not philosophical, but he skims
the surface of philosophy; he is as philosophical
as the House will bear any *effective* orator to be.
He is not poetical, but he can command the
embellishments of poetry, and suits an assembly
which applauds elegance but recoils from imagination. In his deficiencies, therefore—if we
note the limit of the mind—we acknowledge
the skill of the artist—he employs every tool
necessary to his work, and no man with a more
happy effect. To his skill as an orator, he adds

certain rare qualities as a leader; he has little daring, it is true, but he has astonishing tact— he never jeopardizes a party by any rash unto- wardness of phrase—he is free from the indis- cretion habitual to an orator. Another eminent characteristic of his mind is accuracy. I do not remember ever to have heard him misstate a fact,* and I have heard almost every other public speaker misstate a hundred facts. It is probably this constitution of mind which gifts him with his faculty for business. Assuredly no man who, in times of wide and daring specu- lation, pertinaciously resolved to narrow his circle, and be

" Content to live in decencies for ever,"

has been able to invest the existence with more dignity, and to hide with a better effect the limited circumference of his range. There seems to me little doubt but that this accom- plished statesman is enthralled and hampered by the early ties which it is now and henceforth impossible for him, without worldly dishonour, to break. His mind evidently goes beyond the tether of his companions — his arguments are not theirs — to illiberal conclusions he mostly

---

* But he often replies to an *argument* by misstating it wilfully. He is accurate in his own facts, but disingenuous in his reply to the facts advanced by another.

applies liberal reasonings. He describes his narrow circle with compasses disproportionately large, and seems always to act upon that saying of Mirabeau's,—" La politique doit raisonner même sur des suppositions aux quelles elle ne croit pas." It is one of the phenomena of our aristocratic customs, that a man especially marked out by birth and circumstance to be the leader of the popular, should be the defender of the oligarchical party. Sprung from the people, he identifies himself with the patricians. His pure and cold moral character, untinctured by the vices, unseduced by the pursuits of an aristocracy, seems to ally him naturally to the decorous respectabilities of the great middle class to which his connexions attach him ; and even ambition might suggest that his wealth would have made him the first of the one class, though it elevates him to no distinction in the other. Had he placed himself in his natural position among the ranks of the people, he would have been undeniably what he now just fails of being — a GREAT MAN. He would not have been Secretary for Ireland at so early an age, but he would now have been prime minister, or what is a higher position, the leader and centre of the moral power of England. As it is, he has knit himself to a cause which re-

quires passion in its defenders, and is regarded
with suspicion by his allies, because he supports
it with discretion.

You observe then, my friends, that his good
qualities themselves displease and disgust a
large body of the Tories, and they would
adhere to him more zealously if he were less
scrupulous in his politics. For you will readily perceive that, by the more haughty, vehement, and aristocratic of the Tories, *the Whigs
can never be forgiven!* Those who possessed
boroughs, consider themselves robbed of their
property ; those who *zealously* loved the late
form of government, deem themselves defrauded
of a Constitution. Thus insulted self-interest
in some, and even a wounded patriotism in
others, carry the animosities of party into the
obstinacy of revenge. This division of the
Tories care little for your threats of rebellion
or fears of revolution ; they are willing to hazard
any experiment, so discontented are they with the
Present. As the more prudent Tories are chiefly
connected with the trading interest, so the more
daring Tories are mainly connected with the
agricultural ; they rely on their numerous te-
nantry— on their strongholds of clanship and
rustic connexions, with a confidence which
makes them shrink little from even an armed

collision with the people. Claiming amongst
them many of that old indomitable band of
high-born gentry—the true chivalric *noblesse*
of the country, (for to mere titles there are no
ancestral recollections, but blood can bequeath
warlike and exciting traditions,) they are stimulated by the very apprehensions which disarm
the traders. They are instinct with the Black-
wood spirit of resistance; and in that perverted
attachment to freedom, which belongs to an
aristocracy, they deem it equally servile to obey
a people they despise, as to succumb to a ministry they abhor. And of these, many are convinced, surrounded as they are in their visits
to their estates by admiring subordinates, that
their cause is less unpopular and more powerful in mere numerical force than it is represented. How can a Chandos, the idol of his
county, full of courage and of pride, and
equally respected and beloved by the great
agricultural body he represents, — how can *he*
believe you when you tell him that the Tories
are hated ? — how can he listen with patience to
the lukewarm concessions of Sir Robert Peel ?—
to the threats of the Journalists ?—and to the
self-laudatory assertion of the Whigs, that order
and society itself rest solely on their continu-
ance in office ? It is this party, of which,

though he appears but rarely, I consider Lord
Chandos the legitimate and natural head,* that
Sir Robert Peel must perpetually disgust.
Willing to hazard all things to turn out the
ministry, they must naturally divide themselves
from a leader who is willing to concede many
things to keep the ministry in power.

Such is the aspect of the once united and
solid Tory party, — such the character of its
two great divisions, between which the demar-
cation becomes daily more visible and wide.

Turn your eyes now to the ultra Radicals,
what a motley, confused, jarring, miscellany of
irreconcilable theorists! Do two of them think
alike? What connexion is there between the
unvarying Warburton and the contradictory
Cobbett? What harmony betwixt the French
philosophy of this man, and the English prejudices of that? here all is paper money and
passion, there all frigidity and fund-holding.
Each man, ensconced in his own crotchets, is
jealous of the crotchets of the other. Each
man is mad for popularity, and restless for

* I do not mean to say that Lord Chandos is the *acknowledged*
head—for this party have *no* acknowledged head. Perhaps Sir
Edward Knatchbull would be more considered by them than
Lord Chandos. But the latter has only to blame himself if he
be not the leader of his associates. He retires from the field at
the moment he could be most powerful.

position. Vainly would you hope to consoli-
date a great national party that shall embrace
all these discordant materials ; the best we can
do is to incorporate the more reasonable, and
leave the rest as isolated skirmishers, who are
rather useful to harass your enemy, than to
unite with your friends. For do not believe
that all who call themselves your friends are so
in reality; never cease to recollect poor Strap
and the runaway coat-holder !

Turn next to the great ministerial party,
with its body of gold and its feet of clay ; what
a magical chemistry is there not in a treasury
bench ! What scattered particles can it not con-
glomerate ! What antipathetic opposites does it
not combine ! A Palmerston and a Brougham, a
Grant and an Althorp, the wavering indolence
of a Melbourne, and the hardy energies of an
Ellice ! I have read in a quack's advertisement,
that gold may be made the most powerful of
cements— I look to the ministry and I believe it !
The supporters are worthy of the cabinet ; they
are equally various and equally consolidated ;
they shift with the ministers in every turn; bow,
bend, and twist with every government involu-
tion—to-day they repeal a tax, to-morrow restore it ; now they insist on a clause in the Irish
Tithe Bill, as containing its best principle—

and now they erase it as incontestably the most obnoxious; they reflect on the placid stream of their serene subservience every shadow in the April heaven of ministerial supremacy. But we shall find on a more investigating observation, that by the very loyalty of their followers, the Whig ministers are injuring themselves, *" they are dragging their friends through the mire,"* they are directing against them the wrath of their constituents, they are attracting to every sinuosity of creeping complaisance, the indignation and contempt of the country ;— in one homely sentence, *they are endangering the return of their present majority to the next Parliament!* That a Whig majority of one sort or another will be for some years returned by the operations of the Reform Bill, I have before said that I cannot doubt ; but the next majority will be less vast and less confiding than the present! The great failing of the ministers is want of unity,—the Reform Bill united them, and during its progress they were strong; the Reform Bill passed, they had no longer a rallying point; they seem divided in opinion upon every thing else, nay, they allow the misfortune. What mysterious hints do you not hear from every minister, that he is not of the same mind as his brethren. Did not Mr. Stanley declare

VOL. II.

the other night, that on the principle of rendering church property at the disposal of Parliament, he would be disposed to divide on one side, and some of his companions on the other? On what an important question are these declared divisions!

This want of unity betrays itself in all manner of oscillations, the most ludicrous and undignified! Now the ministerial pendulum touches the Mountain Bench; now it vibrates to the crimson seat of his Grace of Wellington. Planning and counter-planning, bowing and explaining, saying and unsaying, bullying to-day and cringing to-morrow, behold the melancholy policy of men who clumsily attempt what Machiavel has termed the finest masterpiece in political science, viz. " to content the people and to manage the nobles."

Pressed by a crowd of jealous and hostile suitors, the only resource of our political Penelopes is in the web that they weave to conciliate each, and unravel in order to baffle all! My friends, as long as a Government lacks unity, believe me it will be ever weak in good, and adherent to mischief. A man must move both legs in order to advance; if one leg stands still, he may flourish with the other to all eternity without stirring a step. We must therefore see if we cannot contrive to impart unity to the Government, should we desire really to progress. How shall we effect this object? It seems to me that we might reasonably hope to effect it in the formation of a new, strong, enlightened, and rational party, on which the Government, in order to retain office, must lean for support. If we could make the ministers as afraid of the House of Commons as they are of the House of Peers, you have no notion how mightily we should brighten their wits and spirit up their measures!

But the most singular infatuation in the present Parliament is, that while ministers are thus daily vacillating from every point in the compass, we are eternally told that we must place unlimited confidence in them. My good friends, is it not only in something firm, steady, and consistent, that any man ever places confidence? — you cannot confide in a vessel that has no rudder, and which one wind drives out of sight, and another wind as suddenly beats back into port. I dare say the ministers are very honest men, I will make no doubt of it. God forbid that I should. I am trustful in human integrity, and I think honesty natural to mankind; but political confidence is given to men not only in proportion to their own honesty, but also in proportion to the circumstances in which they are placed. An individual may repose trust where there is the inclination to fulfil engagement; but the destinies of a people are too grave for such generous credulity. A nation ought only to place its trust where there is no *power* to violate the compact. The difference between confidence in a despotism, and confidence in a representative government, is this: in the former we hope every thing from the virtues of our rulers; in the latter, we would leave nothing we can avoid leaving, to the chance of their errors.

This large demand upon our confidence in men who are never two days the same, is not reasonable or just. *You* have lost that confidence; why should your representatives sacrifice every thing to a shadow, which, like Peter Schemil's, is divorced from its bodily substance —yourselves?

# CHAPTER VII.

A PICTURE OF THE PRESENT HOUSE OF COMMONS.

IT seems, then, that an independent party ought to be formed, strong enough in numbers and in public opinion, to compel the ministers to a firm, a consistent, a liberal, and an independent policy. If so compelled, the Government would acquire unity of course, for those of their present comrades who shrank from that policy which, seemingly the most bold, is in troubled times really the most prudent, would naturally fall off as the policy was pursued. But does the present House of Commons contain materials for the formation of such a party? I think we have reason to hope that it may; there are little less than a hundred members of liberal opinions, yet neither tamely Whig nor fiercely Radical, a proportion of whom are already agreed as to the expediency of such a party, and upon the immediate principles it should attempt to promote. At the early commencement of the first session of the Reformed Parliament such a party ought to have formed itself at once. But to the very name of Party, many had a superstitious objection. Others expected more from the Government than the Government has granted. Some asked who was to be leader; and some thought it a plan that might be *disagreeable to the feelings of Lord Althorp.*

"Rusticus expectat dum defluat amnis."

The stream of time has flowed on, and Rusticus, perhaps, thinks it advisable to wait no longer. As a theory, I dislike the formation of parties. I will show you, my good friends, why, if you wish that independent men shall be useful men, a party at this moment is necessary in practice.

Just walk with me into the House of Commons — there! mount those benches; you are under the Speaker's gallery. The debate is of importance—it is six o'clock—the debate has begun—it goes on very smoothly for an hour or two, during which time most of the members are at dinner, and half the remaining members are asleep. Aware of the advantage of seizing this happy season of tranquillity, some experienced prosers have got the ball of debate in their own hands; they mumble and paw, and toss it about, till near ten o'clock. The House has become full, you resettle yourselves in your seats, you fancy *now* the debate will begin in earnest; those gentlemen who have just entered will give new life to the discussion, they are not tired with the prosing *you* have heard, they come fresh to the field, prepared to listen and applaud. Alas, you are much mistaken! these gentlemen do not come to improve the debate, but to put an end to it as soon as they possibly can. They cluster round the bar in a gloomy galaxy;—like the stars, "they have neither speech nor language, but their voices are heard among them." Hark! a low murmur of question, it creeps, it gathers, and now—a cough! — fatal sound! — a general attack of phthisis seizes upon the House. All the pulmonary diseases of pathology seem suddenly let loose on the unfortunate senators: wheezing and sneezing, and puffing and grunting, till at last the ripening symphony swells into one mighty diapason of simultaneous *groans!* You would think the whole assembly smitten with the plague. Sounds so mournful, so agonizing, so inhuman, and so ghastly, were never heard before! Now and then a solemn voice proclaims " order," a momentary silence succeeds, and then, with a tumultuous reaction, rush once more from nook to nook the unutterable varieties of discord;

" Venti velut agmine facto,
Quà data porta, ruunt, et terras turbine perflant."

But who is the intrepid and patient member, whom at short and dreary intervals you hear

threading with wearied voice the atmosphe-
rical labyrinth of noise. My good friends, it
is an independent member, *he has no party to
back him!* Exhausted and vanquished, the
orator drops at length. Up starts a Tory, dull,
slow, and pompous; the clamour recommences,
it is stopped short by indignant cries of " hear,
hear!" the sound of " order" grows stern and
commanding.

> " Rex Æolus antro
> Luctantes ventos, tempestatesque sonoras
> Imperio premit."

Minister and Tory look round, and by meaning looks enjoin attention from their followers
" for an *old* member of *such* respectability !"
The noisier of the Æolian group escape in
sullen silence through the side doors.

> " Unà Eurusque Notusque ruunt, creberque procellis
> Africus."

And for the next half hour the Tory orator,
with uninterrupted authority, " vexes the dull
ears of the drowsy men." To him succeeds a
Whig, perhaps a Minister; the same silence, and
the same security of prosing. Mark, my friends,
both these gentlemen had a party at their backs !

I assure you that I am a very impartial witness on these facts, and write not at all sorely;
for, being very well contented to be silent, save
when I have any thing to say, I speak but
seldom, as becomes a young member, and at the

early part of the evening among the prosers, as becomes a modest one. It has never therefore been my lot to fall a victim to that ferocity of dissonance which I have attempted to describe. But members more anxious to display their eloquence than I am, have been made so sensible of the impossibility of addressing the House often, without any party to appeal to from the uproarious decisions of the bar, that I believe this cause, more than any other, has driven speech-loving gentlemen into the idea of forming an independent national party. A second reason that has, no doubt, had its weight with them is this: if a member, unsupported by others, bring forward any motion that he considers of importance, he is accused of preventing the business of the night,* and up rises my Lord Althorp, and benevolently puts it to him, whether he will persevere in his motion " against the general sense of the House?" Whereupon the Whigs open their mouths, and emit a considerable cheer. Perhaps the member, if he be

* In order to expedite business, it is a party custom to *count out* the House on an independent member's motion, and so lose a night to the nation. The other day, six gentlemen put off their motions one after another, in order " not to take up the time of the House at so late a period of the session." When all these had thus resigned their right in favour of ministers, what did the House do?—proceed with the ministerial business? No, it adjourned till the next day!

a very bold fellow, perseveringly proceeds, the House being excessively thin and excessively sulky. He sits down, the minister rises, and shuffles the whole question out of discussion, by observing that the honourable gentleman has brought it forward at a time so obviously unfavourable, that, without giving a negative to the principle, he shall think it *(totidem verbis)* his duty to throw as much cold water upon it as he possibly can. The minister having thus discharged his bucket, every Whig member adds a thimbleful ; the cry of question commences by *cock-crow*, and the motion is washed out of the House as fast and as fearfully as if it were poison!

No wonder, my dear friends, that you have been complaining of silence and want of energy in your independent members ; they must have been stubborn spirits indeed, the very Molochs of manhood, to resist such discouraging chills, and such powerful combinations. Depend upon it, that so far as energy and talk are concerned, the independent members will not displease you, if they once resolve to unite. For my part, I have great hopes, should this party be ever properly formed, that the stream will work itself tolerably clear from the muddiness of its source, and that your Reformed Parliament, which disappoints you now, will in a year or two sufficiently content you.

# CHAPTER VIII.

AND what manner of men will they be who shall compose this national party?—My friends, they cannot be the aristocrats. The aristocracy on either side are pledged to old and acknowledged factions, one part to the Tories, another to the Whigs: the party to which I refer must necessarily consist chiefly of new members, and of men wedded to no hereditary affections. So far so well; and what objects will they embrace?—That is more than I can pretend to affirm; but I know what objects they *ought* to embrace.

In the first place, you may remember that in a previous section I observed, that of late years

the intellectual spirit of the time has merged in
the political spirit; so, still more lately, the
political has merged in the economical—you
only think at present of what you can save.
Well, then, a party that shall obtain your opinion and represent your wishes, must consider
economy before all things; not looking to nig-
gard and miserly retrenchments alone, not converting themselves into save-alls of candle-ends
and graters of cheese-parings; but advocating
a vigorous and large retrenchment, extending
from the highest department of state to the
lowest. Never mind what the ministers tell us,
when they say they have done their possible
and can retrench no more. So said the Canning
administration; and yet the Duke of Wellington retrenched some millions. So said the
Duke of Wellington after his retrenchment;
and yet the Whigs have retrenched a few millions more. So say the Whigs now; I fancy,
if we look sharp, and press them hard, that we
shall again find some snug *terra incognita* in
the map of economy—the whole of that chart
is far from being thoroughly explored. Retrenchment should be the first object of this
party,—a retrenchment that shall permit the
repeal of the most oppressive of the taxes, the
assessed taxes, the malt-tax, the stamp duty on

political knowledge. I say boldly RETRENCH-
MENT; for, between you and me, my friends,
I have little faith in the virtue of any commuta-
tion of taxes. I have studied the intricacies
of our finance, I have examined the financial
systems of other countries, and I cannot discover any very large *fiscal* benefit as the probable result of new combinations of taxation.
I own to you that I think you are inclined to
over-rate the merits of a property-tax; depend
upon it that, before such a tax existed three
years, you would be as loud for its repeal as
you are now for the repeal of the house and
window-taxes; *they* are property-taxes,— of a
less just nature, I grant, on the one hand,
but of a less onerous and inquisitorial nature
on the other: — an immense national debt renders direct taxation a dangerous experiment.
No; I should vote for a property-tax, in lieu
of other taxes, merely as a temporary expedient
—as an expedient that would allow us time to
breathe, to look round, to note well what retrenchments we can effect. In a year or two
the retrenchments already made will come more
into sensible operation; in a year or two, if
your minds were made easy on your affairs, quiet
and hope would increase our trade, and therefore
our revenue; in a year or two new savings could

be effected, and the property-tax, if imposed, be swept away : this is the sole benefit I antici- pate from its imposition.  I am for bold and rigid economy, not for its own sake alone, but because I believe, my friends, that, until you get this cursed money-saving out of your heads, until you are sensible that you are fairly treated, and can look at something else than your pockets, you will not be disposed to ex- amine into higher and better principles of go- vernment than its mere cheapness.  In vain pleads the head till the stomach is satisfied ; in vain shall we entreat you to regard your intel- lectual and moral advancement, till we set at rest your anxiety not to be ruined.

Economy, then, should be the first principle of such a party ; but not at that point should its duties be limited.  It is from a profound knowledge of the character of the people to whom legislation is to be applied, that statesmen should legislate.  I have said, in my first book, that the main feature of your character is in- dustry ; industry, therefore, should be support- ed and encouraged.  I have said next, that the *present* disposition of the aristocratic influence weakens and degrades you ; that disposition should be corrected and refined.  I have said, thirdly, that a monarchy is your best preservative from entire deliverance to the domination of brute wealth and oligarchical ascendancy; the monarchy should be strengthened and confirmed. I have said, again, that an established Church preserves you from fanaticism and the worst effects of your constitutional gloom : an established Church should be jealously preserved ; mark me, its preservation does not forbid —no, it necessitates—its reform. I have said that a material and sordid standard of opinion has formed itself in the heart of your commercial tendencies ; and this standard, by organized education, by encouragement to that national spirit which itself gives encouragement to literature, to science, and to art,—by a noble and liberal genius of legislation, we ought to purify and to exalt. This last object neither Whig nor Tory has ever dreamt of effecting. Lord Brougham, indeed, when the Whigs disowned him, comprehended its expediency, and pledged himself to its cause; but, since he has been the member of a Whig cabinet, he seems to have slipped from his principles, and forgotten his pledge. These are the main objects which your national party should have in view. A more vast and a more general object, to which, I fear, no party is yet prepared to apply itself, seems to me to be this,—to merge the names of

People and of Government, to unite them both
in the word STATE. Wherever you see a
good and a salutary constitution, *there* you see
the great masses of the population wedded to
and mingled with the state; there must be
energy to ensure prompt and efficient legislation: energy exists not where unity is wanting.
In Denmark and Prussia is the form of absolute
monarchy; but nowhere are the people hap-
pier or more contented, because in those countries they are utterly amalgamated with the
state, the state protects, and educates, and che-
rishes them all.    In America you behold republicanism; but the state is equally firm as it
is in Denmark or Prussia, the people equally
attached to it, and equally bound up in its existence.    In these opposite constitutions you
behold equal energy, because equal unity.    Antient nations teach us the same truth: in Rome,
in Athens, in Tyre, in Carthage, the people
were strong and prosperous only while the
people and the state were one.    But away with
antient examples! let us come back to common
sense.    Can the mind surrender itself to its
highest exertions when distracted by disquietude
and discontent?    The mind of one individual
reflects the mind of a people, and happiness in
either results from the consciousness of security;

—but you are never secure while you are at variance with your government. In a well-ordered constitution, a constitution in harmony with its subjects, each citizen confounds himself with the state; he is proud that he belongs to it; the genius of the whole people enters into his soul; he is not one man only, he is inspired by the mighty force of the community; he feels the dignity of the nation in himself—he beholds himself in the dignity of the nation. To unite, then, the People and the Government, to prevent that jealousy and antagonism of power which we behold at present, each resisting each to their common weakness, to merge, in one word, both names in the name of State, we must first advance the popular principle to satisfy the people, and then prevent a conceding government by creating a directive one. At present, my friends, you only perceive the Government when it knocks at your door for taxes; you couple with its name the idea not of protection, but of extortion; but I would wish that you should see the Government educating your children, and encouraging your science, and ameliorating the condition of your poor; I wish you to warm while you utter its very name, with a grateful and reverent sense of enlightenment and protection; I wish you to behold all your great Public Blessings repose beneath its shadow; I wish you to feel advancing towards that unceasing and incalculable amelioration which I firmly believe to be the common destiny of mankind, with a steady march and beneath a beloved banner; I wish that every act of a beneficent Reform—should seem to you neither conceded nor extorted,—but as a pledge of a sacred and mutual love;—the legitimate off-spring of one faithful and indissoluble union between the Power of a People and the Majesty of a State!

This is what I mean by a *directive* government; and a government so formed is always strong—strong not for evil, but for good. I know that some imagine that a good government *should* be a weak government, and that the people should thus sway and mould it at their will; you cannot have a weaker government than at present, and I do not see how you are the better for it! But you, the people, do *not* sway a feeble government—I should be delighted if you did; for the people are calm and reasoning, and have a profound sense of the universal interest. But you have a false likeness, my dear friends; a vile, hypocritical, noisy, swaggering fellow, that is usually taken for you, and whom the journalists invariably swear by,—a

creature that is called " THE PUBLIC:" I
know not a more pragmatical, conceited animal
than this said PUBLIC. YOU are immortal,
but the PUBLIC is the grub of a day; he floats
on the mere surface of time; he swallows down
the falsest opinions; he spouts forth the noisiest
fallacies; what he says one hour he unsays the
next; he is a thing of whims and caprices, of
follies and of frenzies. And it is this wrangling
and shallow pretender, it is the Public, and not
the People, that dictates to a feeble government!

You have been misled if you suppose a strong
government is necessarily hostile to you; *coer-
cive* governments are not *strong* ones; governments are never strong save when they suit the
people, but a government truly strong would
be efficient in good; it would curb arrogance as
well as licentiousness. Government was strong
when it carried your Reform Bill through the
House of Lords; Government was weak when
it sacrificed to the Lords the marrow of the
Irish Tithe Bill. An united State, and a strong
Government, — such should be the ulterior objects of a national party really wise and firmly
honest. But the members of such a party
should dismiss all petty ambition, all desire of
office for themselves; they are not strong

enough, for years they cannot be strong
enough, without base and unnatural alliances,
to nourish the hope of coming into power
with the necessary effect. They should limit
their endeavours to retain the best of the present Ministers in office, and to compel them to
a consistent and generous policy. They should
rather imitate the watch-dog, than aspire to the
snug cottage of the shepherd.

This, my friends, is the outline of what, in
my poor opinion, a national party *ought* to be;
but I own to you that when I look to the various component parts of such an association;
when I reflect how difficult it must be to unite
the scruples of some, and to curb the desires of
others, I limit my present hopes to a very small
portion of the benefit it could attain. It is for
you to widen the sphere of that benefit by a
vigilance towards its efforts, and an approbation of its courage. Should it remain unformed
after all—should its elements jar prematurely—
should it dissolve of itself—should it accomplish
none of its objects; and, for want of some such
ground of support to good Government, and of
fear to bad, should our present Ministers continue their oscillatory politics, weakening the
crown, irritating the people, declining to en-
lighten, and incapable to relieve; shifting from

rashness to cowardice, and cowardice to rashness, I behold the most serious cause of apprehension and alarm. I look beyond the day; I see an immense expenditure, an impoverished middle class, an ignorant population, a huge debt, the very magnitude of which tempts to dishonesty; I behold a succession of hasty experiments and legislative quackeries—feuds between the agriculturist * and the fund-holder — " scrambles" at the national purse; tamperings with the currency, and hazardous commutations of taxes; till having run through all the nostrums which Ignorance can administer to the impatience of Disease, we shall come to that last dread operation, of which no man can anticipate the result !

* I firmly believe that if the National Debtor be ever in danger, the fatal attack will come less from the radicals than the country gentlemen, who are jealous of the fund-holder, or crippled with mortgages. The day after the repeal of half of the Malt Tax (leaving a large deficit in the Revenue) was carried, I asked one of its principal supporters, (a popular and independent country gentleman,) how he proposed to repair the deficit?—" By a tax of 2 per cent." quoth he, " upon Master Fund-holder !" — " And if that does not suffice?" asked I.—" Why, then, we must tax him 4 *per cent.*" was the honest rejoinder !

# CHAPTER THE LAST.

### THE AUTHOR'S APOLOGY.

AND now, my dear friends, but little remains for me to say. Your welfare has ever been to me that object, which above all others has excited my ambition, and linked itself with my desires. From my boyhood to this hour, it is to the condition of great masses of men that my interest and my studies have been directed; it is for their amelioration and enlightenment that I have been a labourer and an enthusiast. Yes, I say, enthusiast!—for when a man is sincere, enthusiasm warms him; when useful, enthusiasm directs. Nothing can sustain our hopes for mankind, amidst their own suspicion of our motives and misconstruction of our aims,—amidst the mighty obstacles that oppose every one who struggles with old opinion,—and the innumerable mortifications, that are as the hostile winds of the soul, driving it back upon the haven of torpor and self-seeking;—save that unconquerable and generous zeal which results from a hearty faith in our own honesty, and a

steady conviction of that tendency and power
TO PROGRESS, which the whole history, as well
of Philosophy as of Civilization, assures us to
be the prerogative of our race ! If I have, in
certain broad and determined opinions, separated myself from many of your false and many
of your real friends ; if I have not followed the
more popular leaders of the day against our ecclesiastical establishment, or against a monarchical constitution of government, it is not because
I believe that any minor interests should be consulted before your own ; it is not because I see
a sanctity in hereditary delusions, or in the
solemn austerities of power ; it is not because I
deny that in some conditions of society a republic may be the wisest government,* or be-

* Were I, in this work, giving myself up to the speculative and conjectural philosophy of Politics, I should be
quite willing to allow my conviction that, as yet, we have
scarce passed the threshold of Legislative Science ; and
that vast and organic changes will hereafter take place in
the elements of Government and the social condition of
the World. But I suspect that those changes will be favourable to the concentration, not of power, but the executive *direction* of power, into the *fewest* possible hands ; as
being at once energetic and responsible in proportion to
such a concentration. I think *then* that the Representative System itself will not be found that admirable invention which it is now asserted to be. But these are distant
theories, not adapted to this age, and must be reserved for
the visions of the closet. He *now* is the most useful Po-
litician, who grapples the closest with the time.

cause I maintain that where certain standards
of moral opinion be created, an endowed establishment is necessary to the public virtue; but
it is, because I consider both Institutions subordinate to your welfare; it is because I put
aside the false mists and authorities of the past,
and regard diligently the aspect of the present;
it is because on the one hand I feel persuaded,
viewing the tendencies which belong to our
time, and the moral bias of the general feeling, which, while often seeming to oppose
an aristocracy, inclines equally (in its opposition) to aristocratic fallacies, whether of
wealth or of station, that your republic would
*not* be a true and sound democracy, but the
perpetuater of the worst influences which have
operated on your character and your laws ;—
and because on the other hand, I dread, that the
effects of abolishing an endowed Church would
be less visible in the reform of superstitions,
than in the gloomy advances of fanaticism.   If
I err in these opinions, it is for your sake that
I err; if I am right, let us look with somewhat of prudent jealousy at the declamations
and sarcasms which spring from a partial and
limited survey of the large principles of practical polity; a survey which confounds every
unpopular action of a king with the question of
a monarchy; every failing of a priest, with the

consideration of an establishment; which to-day insinuates a republic, because the King dines with a Tory, and to-morrow denounces an establishment, because a bishop votes against the Whigs.* These are the cries of party, and have no right to response from the more deep and thoughtful sympathies of a nation. Believe me, once more, and once for all, if there be a pretender of whom the People should beware, it is that stage mummer—the Public!

Come what may in the jar and conflict of momentary interests, it is with the permanent and progressive interest of the people, that the

* Whether or not the Bishops should have the privilege to vote in Parliament, is a question I shall not here attempt to decide. For the sake of removing the establishment itself from the perpetual danger of jarring, in its ostensible heads, against the opinions and passions of the people, the privation of that privilege might be desirable, and tend even to the preservation and popularity of the Church; but I beseech the reader to mark that nothing can be more unjust than the present cry against "the time-serving" and "servility" of the episcopal bench! What! when for the first time the prelates have refused all dictation from the Government, have separated themselves wholly from ministerial temptation, have, with obstinate fidelity, clung fast to a falling party, which cannot for years longer than those which usually remain to men who have won to episcopal honours, be restored to power!—what, *now* do you accuse them of time-serving and servility! Alas! it is exactly because they refuse to serve the time; exactly because they abjure servility to the dominant powers, that the public assail and the ministers desert them.

VOL. II.

humble writer who addresses you stands or falls, desiring indeed to proportion your power to your knowledge, but only because believing that all acquisitions of authority, whether by prince or people, which exceed the capacity to preserve and the wisdom to direct, are brief and perilous gains; lost as soon as made; tempting to crude speculations, and ending possibly in ruin. Every imprudence of the popular power is a step to despotism, as every excess of the oligarchical power is the advance of the democratic.

Farewell, my dear friends. We part upon the crisis of unconjecturable events.

> " From this shoal and sand of Time
> We leap the life to come."

Gladly indeed would I pass from dealings with the policy of the present, to the more tempting speculations upon the future; but the sky is uncertain and overcast; and as, my friends, you may observe on a clouded night, that the earth gathers no dew, even so it is not in these dim and unlighted hours that the prophetic thirst of Philosophy may attain to those heavenlier influences which result from a serener sky, and enable her to promise health and freshness to the aspect of the morrow.

# APPENDIX B.

---

### REMARKS ON BENTHAM'S PHILOSOPHY.

IT is no light task to give an abridged view of the philosophical opinions of one, who attempted to place the vast subjects of morals and legislation upon a scientific basis: a mere outline is all that can be attempted.

The first principles of Mr. Bentham's philosophy are these;—that happiness, meaning by that term pleasure and exemption from pain, is the only thing desirable in itself; that all other things are desirable solely as means to that end: that the production, therefore, of the greatest possible happiness, is the only fit purpose of all human thought and action, and consequently of all morality and government; and moreover, that pleasure and pain are the sole agencies by which the conduct of mankind is in fact governed, whatever circumstances the individual may be placed in, and whether he is aware of it or not.

Mr. Bentham does not appear to have entered very deeply into the metaphysical grounds of these doctrines; he seems to have taken those grounds very much upon the showing of the metaphysicians who preceded him. The principle of utility, or as he afterwards called it "the greatest-happiness principle," stands no otherwise demonstrated in his writings, than by an enumeration of the phrases of a different description which have been commonly employed to denote the rule of life, and the rejection of them all, as having no intelligible meaning, further than as they may involve a tacit reference to considerations of utility. Such are the phrases "law of nature," "right reason," "natural rights," "moral sense." All these Mr. Bentham regarded as mere covers for dogmatism; excuses for setting up one's own *ipse dixit* as a rule to bind other people. "They consist, all of them," says he, "in so many contrivances for avoiding the obligation of appealing to any external standard, and for prevailing upon the reader to accept the author's sentiment or opinion as a reason for itself."

This, however, is not fair treatment of the believers in other moral principles than that of utility. All modes of speech are employed in an ignorant manner, by ignorant people; but no one who had thought deeply and systematically enough to be entitled to the name of a philosopher, ever supposed that his *own* private sentiments of approbation and disapprobation must necessarily be well-founded, and needed not to be compared with any external standard. The answer of such persons to Mr. Bentham would be, that by an inductive and analytical examination of the human mind, they had satisfied themselves, that what we call our moral sentiments, (that is, the feelings of complacency and aversion we experience when we compare actions of our own or of other people with our

standard of right and wrong,) are as much part
of the original constitution of man's nature
as the desire of happiness and the fear of suffer-
ing : That those sentiments do not indeed attach
themselves to the same actions under all circumstances, but neither do they, in attaching themselves to actions, follow the law of utility, but
certain other general laws, which are the same in
all mankind naturally ; though education or external circumstances may counteract them, by
creating artificial associations stronger than they.
No proof indeed can be given that we ought to
abide by these laws ; but neither can any proof
be given, that we ought to regulate our conduct
by utility. All that can be said is, that the pursuit of happiness is natural to us ; and so, it is
contended, is the reverence for, and the inclination to square our actions by, certain general
laws of morality.

Any one who is acquainted with the ethical
doctrines either of the Reid and Stewart school,
or of the German metaphysicians (not to go
further back), knows that such would be the
answer of those philosophers to Mr. Bentham ;
and it is an answer of which Mr. Bentham's
writings furnish no sufficient refutation. For
it is evident, that these views of the origin of
moral distinctions are *not*, what he says all such
views are, destitute of any precise and tangible
meaning ; nor chargeable with setting up as a
standard the feelings of the particular person.
They set up as a standard what are assumed (on
grounds which are considered sufficient) to be
the instincts of the species, or principles of our
common nature as universal and inexplicable as
instincts.

To pass judgment on these doctrines, belongs

to a profounder and subtler metaphysics than Mr. Bentham possessed. I apprehend it will be the judgment of posterity, that in his views of what, in the felicitous expression of Hobbes, may be called the *philosophia prima*, it has for the most part, even when he was most completely in the right, been reserved for others to *prove* him so. The greatest of Mr. Bentham's defects, his insufficient knowledge and appreciation of the thoughts of other men, shows itself constantly in his grappling with some delusive shadow of an adversary's opinion, and leaving the actual substance unharmed.

After laying down the principle of Utility, Mr. Bentham is occupied through the most voluminous and the most permanently valuable part of his works, in constructing the outlines of practical ethics and legislation, and filling up some portions of the latter science (or rather art) in great detail; by the uniform and unflinching application of his own greatest-happiness principle, from which the eminently consistent and systematic character of his intellect prevented him from ever swerving. In the writings of no philosopher, probably, are to be detected so few contradictions—so few instances of even momentary deviation from the principles he himself has laid down.

It is perhaps fortunate that Mr. Bentham devoted a much larger share of his time and labour to the subject of legislation, than to that of morals; for the mode in which he understood and applied the principle of Utility, appears to me far more conducive to the attainment of true and valuable results in the former, than in the latter of these two branches of inquiry. The recognition of happiness as the only thing desirable in itself, and of the production of the state of things most favourable to happiness as the only rational end both of morals and policy, by no means necessarily leads to the doctrine of expediency as professed by Paley ; the ethical canon which judges of the morality of an act or a class of actions, solely by the probable *consequences* of that particular kind of act, supposing it to be generally practised. This is a very small part indeed of what a more enlarged understanding of the " greatest-happiness principle" would require us to take into the account. A certain kind of action, as for example, theft, or lying, would, if commonly practised, occasion certain evil consequences to society: but those evil consequences are far from constituting the entire moral bearings of the vices of theft or lying. We shall have a very imperfect view of the relation of those practices to the general happiness, if we suppose them to exist singly, and insulated. All acts suppose certain dispositions, and habits of mind and heart, which may be in themselves states of enjoyment or of wretchedness, and which must be fruitful in *other* consequences, besides those particular acts. No person can be a thief or a liar without being much else : and if our moral judgments and feelings with respect to a person convicted of either vice, were grounded solely upon the pernicious tendency of thieving and of lying, they would be partial and incomplete ; many considerations would be omitted, which are at least equally " germane to the matter ;" many which, by leaving them out of our general views, we may indeed teach ourselves a habit of overlooking, but which it is impossible for any of us not to be

influenced by, in particular cases, in proportion
as they are forced upon our attention.

Now, the great fault I have to find with
Mr. Bentham as a moral philosopher, and the
source of the chief part of the temporary mischief
which in that character, along with a vastly
greater amount of permanent good, he must be
allowed to have produced, is this : that he has
practically, to a very great extent, confounded
the principle of Utility with the principle of
specific consequences, and has habitually made
up his estimate of the approbation or blame
due to a particular kind of action, from a
calculation solely of the consequences to which
that very action, if practised generally, would
itself lead. He has largely exemplified, and
contributed very widely to diffuse, a tone of
thinking, according to which any kind of action
or any habit, which in its own specific consequences cannot be proved to be necessarily
or probably productive of unhappiness to the
agent himself or to others, is supposed to be
fully justified ; and any disapprobation or aversion entertained towards the individual by
reason of it, is set down from that time forward as prejudice and superstition. It is not
considered (at least, not habitually considered,)
whether the act or habit in question, though
not in itself necessarily pernicious, may not
form part of a *character* essentially pernicious,
or at least essentially deficient in some quality
eminently conducive to the " greatest happiness." To apply such a standard as this, would
indeed often require a much deeper insight into
the formation of character, and knowledge of the
internal workings of human nature, than Mr.
Bentham possessed. But, in a greater or less

degree, he, and every one else, judges by this
standard : even those who are warped, by some
partial view, into the omission of all such elements from their general speculations.

When the moralist thus overlooks the relation
of an act to a certain state of mind as its cause,
and its connexion through that common cause
with large classes and groups of actions apparently very little resembling itself, his estimation even of the consequences of the very act
itself, is rendered imperfect. For it may be
affirmed with few exceptions, that any act whatever has a tendency to fix and perpetuate the
state or character of mind in which itself has originated. And if that important element in the
moral relations of the action be not taken into account by the moralist as a cause, neither probably will it be taken into account as a consequence.

Mr. Bentham is far from having altogether
overlooked this side of the subject. Indeed,
those most original and instructive, though, as
I conceive, in their spirit, partially erroneous
chapters, on *motives* and on *dispositions*, in his
first great work, the Introduction to the Principles of Morals and Legislation, open up a direct
and broad path to these most important topics.
It is not the less true that Mr. Bentham, and
many others, following his example, when they
came to discuss particular questions of ethics,
have commonly, in the superior stress which they
laid upon the specific consequences of a class of
acts, rejected all contemplation of the action in its
general bearings upon the entire moral being of
the agent ; or have, to say the least, thrown those
considerations so far into the background, as
to be almost out of sight. And by so doing they
have not only marred the value of many of their

speculations, considered as mere philosophical
enquiries, but have always run the risk of incur-
ring, and in many cases have in my opinion
actually incurred, serious practical errors.

This incompleteness, however, in Mr. Bentham's general views, was not of a nature materially to diminish the value of his speculations
through the greater part of the field of legislation.
Those of the bearings of an action, upon which
Mr. Bentham bestowed almost exclusive attention, were also those with which almost alone
legislation is conversant. The legislator en-
joins or prohibits an action, with very little regard to the general moral excellence or turpitude
which it implies; he looks to the consequences to
society of the particular kind of action ; his object is not to render people incapable of *desiring*
a crime, but to deter them from actually *committing* it. Taking human beings as he finds
them, he endeavours to supply such inducements as will constrain even persons of the dispositions the most at variance with the general
happiness, to practise as great a degree of regard to it in their actual conduct, as can be obtained from them by such means without preponderant inconvenience. A theory, therefore,
which considers little in an action besides that
action's *own* consequences, will generally be sufficient to serve the purposes of a philosophy of
legislation. Such a philosophy will be most apt
to fail in the consideration of the greater social
questions — the theory of organic institutions
and general forms of polity ; for those (unlike
the details of legislation) to be duly estimated,
must be viewed as the great instruments of
forming the national character ; of carrying
forward the members of the community towards

perfection, or preserving them from degeneracy.
This, as might in some measure be expected, is
a point of view in which, except for some partial or limited purpose, Mr. Bentham seldom
contemplates these questions. And this signal
omission is one of the greatest of the deficiencies
by which his speculations on the theory of government, though full of valuable ideas, are
rendered, in my judgment, altogether incon-
clusive in their general results.

To these we shall advert more fully hereafter. As yet I have not acquitted myself of
the more agreeable task of setting forth some
part of the services which the philosophy of
legislation owes to Mr. Bentham.

The greatest service of all, that for which posterity will award most honour to his name, is one
that is his exclusively, and can be shared by no
one present or to come ; it is the service which
can be performed only once for any science, that
of pointing out by what method of investigation
it may be *made* a science. What Bacon did for
physical knowledge, Mr. Bentham has done for
philosophical legislation. Before Bacon's time,
many physical facts had been ascertained ; and
previously to Mr. Bentham, mankind were in
possession of many just and valuable detached
observations on the making of laws. But he
was the first who attempted regularly to deduce
all the secondary and intermediate principles of
law, by direct and systematic inference from the
one great axiom or principle of general utility.
In all existing systems of law, those secondary
principles or dicta in which the essence of the
systems resided, had grown up in detail, and
even when founded in views of utility, were not
the result of any scientific and comprehensive

course of enquiry; but more frequently were purely technical; that is, they had grown out of circumstances purely *historical*, and, not having been altered when those circumstances changed, had nothing left to rest upon but fictions, and unmeaning forms. Take for instance the law of real property; the whole of which continues to this very day to be founded on the doctrine of feudal tenures, when those tenures have long ceased to exist except in the phraseology of Westminster Hall. Nor was the *theory* of law in a better state than the practical systems; speculative jurists having dared little more than to refine somewhat upon the technical maxims of the particular body of jurisprudence which they happened to have studied. Mr. Bentham was the first who had the genius and courage to conceive the idea of bringing back the science to first principles. This could not be done, could scarcely even be attempted, without, as a necessary consequence, making obvious the utter worthlessness of many, and the crudity and want of precision of almost all, the maxims which had previously passed everywhere for principles of law.

Mr. Bentham, moreover, has warred against the errors of existing systems of jurisprudence, in a more direct manner than by merely presenting the contrary truths. The force of argument with which he rent asunder the fantastic and illogical maxims on which the various technical systems are founded, and exposed the flagrant evils which they practically produce, is only equalled by the pungent sarcasm and exquisite humour with which he has derided their absurdities, and the eloquent declamation which he continually pours forth against them, sometimes in the form of lamentation, and sometimes of invective.

This, then, was the first, and perhaps the grandest achievement of Mr. Bentham ; the entire discrediting of all technical systems ; and the example which he set of treating law as no peculiar mystery, but a simple piece of practical business, wherein means were to be adapted to ends, as in any of the other arts of life. To have accomplished this, supposing him to have done nothing else, is to have equalled the glory of the greatest scientific benefactors of the human race.

But Mr. Bentham, unlike Bacon, did not merely prophesy a science ; he made large strides towards the creation of one. He was the first who conceived with anything approaching to precision, the idea of a Code, or complete body of law ; and the distinctive characters of its essential parts,—the Civil Law, the Penal Law, and the Law of Procedure. On the first two of these three departments he rendered valuable service ; the third he actually created. Conformably to the habits of his mind, he set about investigating *ab initio*, a philosophy or science for each of the three branches. He did with the received principles of each, what a good code would do with the laws themselves ; — extirpated the bad, substituting others ; re-enacted the good, but in so much clearer and more methodical a form, that those who were most familiar with them before, scarcely recognized them as the same. Even upon old truths, when they pass through his hands, he leaves so many of his marks, that often he almost seems to claim the discovery of what he has only systematized.

In creating the philosophy of Civil Law, he
proceeded not much beyond establishing on the
proper basis some of its most general principles,
and cursorily discussing some of the most interesting of its details. Nearly the whole of
what he has published on this branch of law, is
contained in the *Traités de Législation*, edited
by M. Dumont. To the most difficult part,
and that which most needed a master-hand to
clear away its difficulties, the nomenclature and
arrangement of the Civil Code, he contributed
little, except detached observations, and criticisms upon the errors of his predecessors. The
" Vue Générale d'un Corps Complet de Législation," included in the work just cited, contains almost all which he has given to us on
this subject.

In the department of Penal Law, he is the
author of the best attempt yet made towards a
philosophical classification of offences. The
theory of punishments (for which however
more had been done by his predecessors, than
for any other part of the science of law) he left
nearly complete.

The theory of Procedure (including that of
the constitution of the courts of justice) he
found in a more utterly barbarous state than
even either of the other branches ; and he left
it incomparably the most perfect. There is
scarcely a question of practical importance in
this most important department, which he has
not settled. He has left next to nothing for his
successors.

He has shown with the force of demonstra-
tion, and has enforced and illustrated the truth
in a hundred ways, that by sweeping away the
greater part of the artificial rules and forms

which obtain in all the countries called civilized, and adopting the simple and direct modes of investigation, which all men employ in endeavouring to ascertain facts for their own private knowledge, it is possible to get rid of at least nine-tenths of the expense, and ninety-nine hundredths of the delay, of law proceedings; not only with no increase, but with an almost incredible diminution, of the chances of erroneous decision. He has also established irrefragably the principles of a good judicial establishment: a division of the country into districts, with *one* judge in each, appointed only for a limited period, and deciding all sorts of cases; with a deputy under him, appointed and removable by himself: an appeal lying in all cases whatever, but by the transmission of papers only, to a supreme court or courts, consisting each of only *one* judge, and stationed in the metropolis.

It is impossible within the compass of this sketch, to attempt any further statement of Mr. Bentham's principles and views on the great science which first became a science in his hands.

As an analyst of human nature (the faculty in which above all it is necessary that an ethical philosopher should excel) I cannot rank Mr. Bentham very high. He has done little in this department, beyond introducing what appears to me a very deceptive phraseology, and furnishing a catalogue of the " springs of action," from which some of the most important are left out.

That the actions of sentient beings are wholly determined by pleasure and pain, is the fundamental principle from which he starts; and thereupon Mr. Bentham creates a *motive*, and an *interest*, corresponding to each pleasure or pain, and affirms that our actions are determined by our *interests*, by the *preponderant* interest, by the *balance* of motives. Now if this only means what was before asserted, that our actions are determined by pleasure and pain, that simple and unambiguous mode of stating the proposition is preferable. But under cover of the obscurer phrase a meaning creeps in, both to the author's mind and the reader's, which goes much farther, and is entirely false: that all our acts are determined by pains and pleasures *in prospect*, pains and pleasures to which we look forward as the *consequences* of our acts. This, as a universal truth, can in no way be maintained. The pain or pleasure which determines our conduct is as frequently one which *precedes* the moment of action as one which follows it. A man *may*, it is true, be deterred, in circumstances of temptation, from perpetrating a crime, by his dread of the punishment, or of the remorse, which he fears he may have to endure *after* the guilty act; and in that case we may say with some kind of propriety, that his conduct is swayed by the balance of motives; or, if you will, of interests. But the case *may* be, and is to the full as likely to be, that he recoils from the very thought of committing the act; the idea of placing himself in such a situation is so painful, that he cannot dwell upon it long enough to have even the physical power of perpetrating the crime. His conduct is determined by pain; but by a pain which precedes the act, not by one which is expected to follow it. Not only *may* this be so, but unless it be so, the man is not really virtuous. The fear of pain *consequent* upon the act, cannot arise, unless there be *deliberation*; and the man

as well as " the woman who deliberates," is in
imminent danger of being lost. With what propriety shrinking from an action without deliberation, can be called yielding to an *interest*, I
cannot see. *Interest* surely conveys, and is intended to convey, the idea of an *end*, to which
the conduct (whether it be act or forbearance)
is designed as the *means*. Nothing of this sort
takes place in the above example. It would be
more correct to say that conduct is *sometimes*
determined by an *interest*, that is, by a deliberate
and conscious aim ; and sometimes by an *impulse*, that is, by a feeling (call it an association
if you think fit) which has no ulterior end, the
act or forbearance becoming an end in itself.

The attempt, again, to *enumerate* motives,
that is, human desires and aversions, seems to
me to be in its very conception an error. Motives are innumerable : there is nothing whatever which may not become an object of desire or of dislike by association. It may be desirable to distinguish by peculiar notice the
motives which are strongest and of most frequent operation ; but Mr. Bentham has not
even done this. In his list of motives, though
he includes sympathy, he omits conscience, or
the feeling of duty : one would never imagine
from reading him that any human being ever
did an act merely because it is right, or abstain-
ed from it merely because it is wrong. In this
Mr. Bentham differs widely from Hartley, who,
although he considers the moral sentiments to
be wholly the result of association, does not
therefore deny them a place in his system,
but includes the feelings of " the moral sense"
as one of the six classes into which he divides
pleasures and pains. In Mr. Bentham's own

mind, deeply imbued as it was with the " greatest-happiness principle, " this motive was probably so blended with that of sympathy as to be undistinguishable from it ; but he should have recollected that those who acknowledge another standard of right and wrong than happiness, or who have never reflected on the subject at all, have often very strong feelings of moral obligation ; and whether a person's standard be happiness or anything else, his attachment to his standard is not necessarily in proportion to his benevolence. Persons of weak sympathies have often a strong feeling of justice ; and others, again, with the feelings of benevolence in considerable strength, have scarcely any consciousness of moral obligation at all.

It is scarcely necessary to point out that the habitual omission of so important a spring of action in an enumeration professing to be complete, must tend to create a habit of overlooking the same phenomenon, and consequently making no allowance for it, in other moral speculations. It is difficult to imagine any more fruitful source of gross error ; though one would be apt to suppose the oversight an impossible one, without this evidence of its having been committed by one of the greatest thinkers our species has produced. How can we suppose him to be alive to the existence and force of the motive in particular cases, who omits it in a deliberate and comprehensive enumeration of all the influences by which human conduct is governed ?

In laying down as a philosophical axiom, that men's actions are always obedient to their interests, Mr. Bentham did no more than dress

up the very trivial proposition that all persons
do what they feel themselves most disposed
to do, in terms which appeared to him more
precise, and better suited to the purposes of
philosophy, than those more familiar expressions. He by no means intended by this assertion to impute universal selfishness to mankind, for he reckoned the motive of sympathy
as an *interest*, and would have included conscience under the same appellation, if that
motive had found any place in his philosophy, as a distinct principle from benevolence.
He distinguished two kinds of interests, the
self-regarding and the social : in vulgar dis-
course, the name is restricted to the former
kind alone.

But there cannot be a greater mistake
than to suppose that, because we may ourselves be perfectly *conscious* of an ambiguity
in our language, that ambiguity therefore has
no effect in perverting our modes of thought.
I am persuaded, from experience, that this
habit of speaking of all the feelings which
govern mankind under the name of *interests*,
is almost always in point of fact connected
with a tendency to consider *interest* in the
vulgar sense, that is, purely self-regarding
interest, as exercising, by the very constitution
of human nature, a far more exclusive and
paramount control over human actions than it
really does exercise. Such, certainly, was the
tendency of Mr. Bentham's own opinions. Habitually, and throughout his works, the moment
he has shown that a man's *selfish* interest
would prompt him to a particular course of
action, he lays it down without further parley
that the man's interest lies that way ; and,

by sliding insensibly from the vulgar sense of the word into the philosophical, and from the philosophical back into the vulgar, the conclusion which is always brought out is, that the man will act as the selfish interest prompts. The extent to which Mr. Bentham was a believer in the predominance of the selfish principle in human nature, may be seen from the sweeping terms in which, in his Book of Fallacies, he expressly lays down that predominance as a philosophical axiom.

" In *every* human breast (rare and short-lived ebullitions, the result of some extraordinarily strong stimulus or excitement, excepted) self-regarding interest is predominant over social interest ; each person's own individual interest over the interests of all other persons taken together." pp. 392–3.

In another passage of the same work (p. 363) he says, " Taking the whole of life together, there exists not, *nor ever can exist,* that human being in whose instance any public interest he can have had will not, in so far as depends upon himself, have been sacrificed to his own personal interest. Towards the advancement of the public interest, all that the most public-spirited (which is as much as to say the most virtuous) of men can do, is to do what depends upon himself towards bringing the public interest, that is, his own personal share in the public interest, to a state as nearly approaching to coincidence, and on as few occasions amounting to a state of repugnance, as possible, with his private interests."

By the promulgation of such views of human nature, and by a general tone of thought and expression perfectly in harmony with them,

I conceive Mr. Bentham's writings to have done and to be doing very serious evil. It is by such things that the more enthusiastic and generous minds are prejudiced against all his other speculations, and against the very attempt to make ethics and politics a subject of precise and philosophical thinking ; which attempt, indeed, if it were necessarily connected with such views, would be still more pernicious than the vague and flashy declamation for which it is proposed as a substitute. The effect is still worse on the minds of those who are not shocked and repelled by this tone of thinking, for on them it must be perverting to their whole moral nature. It is difficult to form the conception of a tendency more inconsistent with all rational hope of good for the human species, than that which must be impressed by such doctrines, upon any mind in which they find acceptance.

There are, there have been, many human beings, in whom the motives of patriotism or of benevolence have been permanent steady principles of action, superior to any ordinary, and in not a few instances, to any possible, temptations of personal interest. There are, and have been, multitudes, in whom the motive of conscience or moral obligation has been thus paramount. There is nothing in the constitution of human nature to forbid its being so in all mankind. Until it is so, the race will never enjoy one-tenth part of the happiness which our nature is susceptible of. I regard any considerable increase of human happiness, through mere changes in outward circumstances, unaccompanied by changes in the state of the desires, as hopeless ; not to mention that while the desires are circum-

scribed in self, there can be no adequate motive
for exertions tending to modify to good ends
even those external circumstances. No man's
individual share of any public good which he
can hope to realize by his efforts, is an equi-
valent for the sacrifice of his ease, and of the
personal objects which he might attain by another course of conduct. The balance can be
turned in favour of virtuous exertion, only by
the interest of *feeling* or by that of *conscience*—
those "social interests," the necessary subordina-
tion of which to " self-regarding " is so lightly
assumed.

But the power of any one to realize in himself
the state of mind, without which his own enjoyment of life can be but poor and scanty, and
on which all our hopes of happiness or moral
perfection to the species must rest, depends entirely upon his having faith in the actual existence of such feelings and dispositions in others,
and in their possibility for himself. It is for
those in whom the feelings of virtue are weak,
that ethical writing is chiefly needful, and its
proper office is to strengthen those feelings.
But to be qualified for this task, it is necessary,
first to have, and next to show, in every sentence
and in every line, a firm unwavering confidence
in man's capability of virtue. It is by a sort of
sympathetic contagion, or inspiration, that a
noble mind assimilates other minds to itself;
and no one was ever inspired by one whose
own inspiration was not sufficient to give him
faith in the possibility of making others feel
what *he* feels.

Upon those who *need* to be strengthened and
upheld by a really inspired moralist — such a
moralist as Socrates, or Plato, or (speaking
humanly and not theologically) as Christ; the

effect of such writings as Mr. Bentham's, if they be read and believed and their spirit imbibed, must either be hopeless despondency and gloom, or a reckless giving themselves up to a life of that miserable self-seeking, which they are there taught to regard as inherent in their original and unalterable nature.

Mr. Bentham's speculations on politics in the narrow sense, that is, on the theory of government, are distinguished by his usual characteristic, that of beginning at the beginning. He places before himself man in society without a government, and, considering what sort of government it would be advisable to construct, finds that the most expedient would be a representative democracy. Whatever may be the value of this conclusion, the mode in which it is arrived at appears to me to be fallacious; for it assumes that mankind are alike in all times and all places, that they have the same wants and are exposed to the same evils, and that if the same institutions do not suit them, it is only because in the more backward stages of improvement they have not wisdom to see what institutions are most for their good. How to invest certain servants of the people with the power necessary for the protection of person and property, with the greatest possible facility to the people of changing the depositaries of that power, when they think it is abused; such is the only problem in social organization which Mr. Bentham has proposed to himself. Yet this is but a part of the real problem. It never seems to have occurred to him to regard political institutions in a higher light, as the principal means of the social education of a people. Had he done so, he would have seen that the same institutions will no more suit two nations in different stages of civilization, than the same lessons will suit children of different ages. As the degree of civilization already attained varies, so does the kind of social influence necessary for carrying the community forward to the next stage of its progress. For a tribe of North American Indians, improvement means, taming down their proud and solitary self-dependence; for a body of emancipated negroes, it means accustoming them to be self-dependent, instead of being merely obedient to orders: for our semi-barbarous ancestors it would have meant, softening them; for a race of enervated Asiatics it would mean hardening them. How can the same social organization be fitted for producing so many contrary effects?

The prevailing error of Mr. Bentham's views of human nature appears to me to be this—he supposes mankind to be swayed by only a part of the inducements which really actuate them; but of that part he imagines them to be much cooler and more thoughtful calculators than they really are. He has, I think, been, to a certain extent, misled in the theory of politics, by supposing that the submission of the mass of mankind to an established government is mainly owing to a reasoning perception of the necessity of legal protection, and of the common interest of all in a prompt and zealous obedience to the law. He was not, I am persuaded, aware, how very much of the really wonderful acquiescence of mankind in any government which they find established, is the effect of mere habit and imagination, and, therefore, depends upon the preservation of something like continuity of existence in the institutions, and identity in their outward forms; cannot transfer itself easily to new in-

stitutions, even though in themselves preferable; and is greatly shaken when there occurs
anything like a break in the line of historical duration—anything which can be termed
the end of the old constitution and the beginning of a new one.

The constitutional writers of our own country, anterior to Mr. Bentham, had carried feelings of this kind to the height of a superstition;
they never considered what was best adapted
to their own times, but only what had existed
in former times, even in times that had long
gone by. It is not very many years since such
were the principal grounds on which parliamentary reform itself was defended. Mr. Bentham has done much service in discrediting,
as he has done completely, this school of politicians, and exposing the absurd sacrifice of
present ends to antiquated means; but he has, I
think, himself fallen into a contrary error. The
very fact that a certain set of political institutions already exist, have long existed, and
have become associated with all the historical
recollections of a people, is in itself, as far as it
goes, a property which adapts them to that
people, and gives them a great advantage over
any new institutions in obtaining that ready
and willing resignation to what has once been
decided by lawful authority, which alone renders possible those innumerable compromises
between adverse interests and expectations,
without which no government could be carried
on for a year, and with difficulty even for a
week. Of the perception of this important
truth, scarcely a trace is visible in Mr. Bentham's writings.*

* It is necessary, however, to distinguish between Mr.
Bentham's practical conclusions, as an English politi-

It is impossible, however, to contest to Mr. Bentham, on this subject or on any other which he has touched, the merit, and it is very great, of having brought forward into notice one of the faces of the truth, and a highly important one. Whether on government, on morals, or on any of the other topics on which his speculations are comparatively imperfect, they are still highly instructive and valuable to any one who is capable of supplying the remainder of the truth ; they are calculated to mislead only by the pretension which they invariably set up of being the whole truth, a complete theory and philosophy of the subject. Mr. Bentham was more a thinker than a reader ; he seldom compared his ideas with those of other philosophers, and was by no means aware how many thoughts had existed in other minds, which his doctrines did not afford the means either to refute or to appreciate.

cian of the present day, and his systematic views as a political philosopher. It is to the latter only that the foregoing observations are intended to apply: on the former I am not now called upon to pronounce any opinion. For the just estimation of his merits, the question is not what were his conclusions, but what was his mode of arriving at them. Theoretical views most widely different, may lead to the same practical corollaries : and that part of any system of philosophy which bodies itself forth in directions for immediate practice, must be so small a portion of the whole as to furnish a very insufficient criterion of the degree in which it approximates to scientific and universal truth. Let Mr. Bentham's opinions on the political questions of the day be as sound or as mistaken as any one may deem them, the fact which is of importance in judging of Mr. Bentham himself is that those opinions rest upon a basis of half-truth. Each enquirer is left to add the other half for himself, and confirm or correct the practical conclusion as the other lights of which he happens to be in possession, allow him.

# APPENDIX C.

### A FEW OBSERVATIONS ON MR. MILL.

Mr. Mill has been frequently represented as the disciple of Bentham. With truth has he been so represented in this respect—he was one of the earliest in adopting—he has been one of the most efficient in diffusing—many of the most characteristic of Bentham's opinions. He admits without qualification—he carries into detail with rigid inflexibility, the doctrine that the sole ground of moral obligation is *general utility*. But the same results may be reached by minds the most dissimilar; else why do we hope for agreement amongst impartial inquirers? —else why do we hope to convert one another? why not burn our lucubrations, or wait to establish a principle until we have found an exact resemblance of ourselves?

In some respects Mr. Mill's mind assimilates to Bentham's, in others it differs from it widely. It is true that Mr. Mill's speculations have been influenced by impressions received from Bentham; but they have been equally influenced by those received from the Aristotelian Logicians, from Hartley, and from Hobbes. He almost alone in the present age has revived the study of those writers—he has preserved, perhaps, the

most valuable of their doctrines—he is largely
indebted to them for the doctrines which compose, for the spirit which pervades his philosophy. The character of his intellect seems to partake as much of that of either of those three
types of speculative inquiry, as it does of the
likeness of Bentham.

As a searcher into original truths, the principal contribution which Mr. Mill has rendered
to philosophy, is to be found in his most recent
work, " The Analysis of the Phenomena of
the Human Mind." Nothing more clearly
proves what I have before asserted, viz.—our
indifference to the higher kind of philosophical
investigation, than the fact, that no full account
—no *criticism* of this work has appeared in
either of our principal Reviews.

The doctrine announced by Hartley, that the
ideas furnished by Sense, together with the law
of association, are the simple elements of the
mind, and sufficient to explain even the most
mysterious of its phenomena, is also the doctrine of Mr. Mill. Hartley, upon this principle, had furnished an explanation of *some* of
the phenomena. Mr. Mill has carried on the investigation into all those more complex psycho-
logical facts which had been the puzzle and despair of previous metaphysicians. Such, for instance, as Time and Space—Belief—the Will—
the Affections—the Moral Sentiments. He has
attempted to resolve all these into cases of association. I do not pause here to contend with
him—to show, or rather endeavour to show,
where he has succeeded—where failed. It would
be a task far beyond the limits of this Book—it
is properly the task of future metaphysicians.

The moment in which this remarkable work
appeared is unfortunate for its temporary suc-

cess. Had it been published sixty years ago—
or perhaps sixty years hence, it would perhaps
have placed the reputation of its author beyond
any of his previous writings.

There is nothing similar to these inquiries in
the writings of Mr. Bentham. This indicates
one principal difference between the two men.
Mr. Mill is eminently a metaphysician; Bentham as little of a metaphysician as any one can
be who ever attained to equal success in the
science of philosophy. Every moral or political system must be indeed a corollary from
some general view of human nature. But Bentham, though punctilious and precise in the
premises he advances, confines himself, in that
very preciseness, to a few simple and general
principles. *He seldom analyses*—he studies the
human mind rather after the method of natural
history than of philosophy. He enumerates—he
classifies the facts—but he does not *account* for
them. You read in his works an enumeration
of pains and pleasures—an enumeration of motives—an enumeration of the properties which
constitute the value of a pleasure or a pain.
But Bentham does not even attempt to *explain*
any of the feelings or impulses enumerated—he
does not attempt to show that they are subject
to the laws of any more elementary phenomena
of human nature. Of human nature indeed in its
rarer or more hidden parts, Bentham knew but
little—wherever he attained to valuable results,
which his predecessors had missed, it was by
estimating more justly than they the action of
some outward circumstance upon the more obvious and vulgar elements of our nature—not by
understanding better than they, the workings of
those elements which are not obvious and not
vulgar. Where but a moderate knowledge of

these last was necessary to the correctness of his conclusions, he was apt to stray farther from the truth than even the votaries of common place. He often threw aside a trite and unsatisfactory truism, in order to replace it with a paradoxical error.

If, then, the power of analysing a complex combination into its simple elements be in the mental sciences, as in the physical, a leading characteristic of the philosopher, Mr. Mill is thus far considerably nearer to the philosophic ideal than Mr. Bentham. This, however, has not made so great a difference as might have been expected in the practical conclusions at which they have arrived. Those powers of analysis which, by Mr. Bentham, are not brought to bear upon the phenomena of our nature at all, are applied by Mr. Mill almost solely to our *common universal* nature, to the general structure which is the same in all human beings; not to the differences between one human being and another, though the former is little worthy of being studied except as a means to the better understanding of the latter. We seldom learn from Mr. Mill to understand any of the varieties of human nature; and, in truth, they enter very little into his own calculations, except where he takes cognizance of them as aberrations from the standard to which, in his opinion, all should conform. Perhaps there never existed any writer, (except, indeed, the ascetic theologians,) who conceived the excellence of the human being so exclusively under one single type, to a conformity with which he would reduce all mankind. No one ever made fewer allowances for original differences of nature, although the existence of such is not only compatible with, but a necessary consequence of, his view of the

human mind, when combined with the extraordinary differences which are known to exist between one individual and another in the kind and in the degree of their nervous sensibility. I cannot but think that the very laws of association, laid down by Mr. Mill, will hereafter, and in other hands, be found (while they explain the diversities of human nature) to show, in the most striking manner, how much of those diversities is inherent and inevitable; neither the effect of, nor capable of being reached by, education or outward circumstances.*
I believe the natural and necessary differences among mankind to be so great, that any practical view of human life, which does not take them into the account, must, unless it stop short in generalities, contain at least as much error as truth; and that any system of mental culture, recommended by such imperfect theory in proportion as it is fitted to natures of one class, will be entirely unfitted for all others.

Mr. Mill has given to the world, as yet, on the subject of morals, and on that of education, little besides generalities: not "barren generalities," but of the most fruitful kind; yet of which the fruit is still to come. When he shall carry his speculations into the details of these subjects, it is impossible that an intellect like his should not throw a great increase of light upon them: the danger is that the illumination will be partial and narrow; that he will conclude too readily that, whatever is suitable food for one sort of character, or suitable medicine for bringing it back, when it falls from its

* I venture to recommend to the notice of the Reader an able paper on the character of Dr. Priestley, published in several recent numbers of Mr. Fox's excellent Monthly Repository.

proper excellence, may be prescribed for *all*, and that what is *not* needful or useful to one of the types of human nature, is worthless altogether. There is yet another danger, that he will fail, not only in conceiving sufficient variety of excellence, but sufficiently *high* excellence ; that the type to which he would reduce all natures, is by no means the most perfect type ; that he conceives the ideal perfection of a human being, under *some* only of its aspects, not under all ; or at least that he would frame his practical rules as if he so conceived it.

The faculty of drawing correct conclusions from evidence, together with the qualities of moral rectitude and earnestness, seems to constitute almost the whole of his idea of the perfection of human nature ; or rather, he seems to think, that with all other valuable qualities mankind are already sufficiently provided, or will be so by attending merely to these. We see no provision in his system, so far as it is disclosed to us, for the cultivation of any other qualities ; and therefore, (as I hold to be a necessary consequence,) no *sufficient* provision for the cultivation even of these.

Now there are few persons whose notion of the perfection to which a human being may be brought, does not comprehend much more than the qualities enumerated above. Most will be prepared to find the practical views founded upon so narrow a basis of theory, rather fit to be used as part of the materials for a practical system, than fit in themselves to constitute one. From what cause, or combination of causes, the scope of Mr. Mill's philosophy embraces so partial a view only of the ends of human culture and of human life, it belongs rather to Mr. Mill's biographer than to his mere reader, to investigate. Doubtless the views of almost all inquirers into human nature are necessarily confined within certain bounds by the fact, that they can enjoy complete power of studying their subject only as it exists in themselves. No person can thoroughly appreciate that of which he has not had personal consciousness: but powers of metaphysical analysis, such as Mr. Mill possesses, are sufficient for the understanding and appreciation of all characters and all states of mind, as far as is necessary for practical purposes, and amply sufficient to divest our philosophic theories of everything like narrowness. For this, however, it is necessary that those powers of analysis should be applied to the details, not solely to the outlines, of human nature; and one of the most strongly marked of the mental peculiarities of Mr. Mill, is, as it seems to us, impatience of details.

This is another of the most striking differences between him and Mr. Bentham. Mr. Bentham delighted in details, and had a quite extraordinary genius for them: it is remarkable how much of his intellectual superiority was of this kind. He followed out his inquiries into the minutest ramifications; was skilful in the estimation of small circumstances, and most sagacious and inventive in devising small contrivances. He went even to great excess in the time and labour which he was willing to bestow on minutiæ, when more important things remained undone. Mr. Mill, on the contrary, shuns all nice attention to details; he attaches himself exclusively to great and leading points; his views, even when they cannot be said to be enlarged, are always on a large scale. He will often be thought by those who differ from him, to overlook or undervalue great things,—never to exaggerate small ones; and the former, partly from not being attentive *enough* to details, when these, though small, would have suggested principles which are great.

The same undervaluing of details has, I think, caused most of the imperfections, where imperfections there are, in Mr. Mill's speculations generally. His just contempt of those who are incapable of grasping a general truth, and with whom the grand and determining considerations are always outweighed by some petty circumstance, carries him occasionally into an opposite extreme: he so heartily despises those most obtuse persons who call themselves Practical Men, and disavow theory, as not always to recollect that, though the men be purblind, they may yet "look out upon the world with their dim horn eyes" and see something in it, which, lying out of his way, he may not have observed, but which it may be worth while for him, who *can* see clearly, to note and *explain*. Not only a dunce may give instruction to a wise man, but no man is so wise that he can, in all cases, do without a dunce's assistance. But a certain degree of intellectual impatience is almost necessarily connected with fervour of character and strength of conviction. Men much inferior to Mr. Mill are quite capable of setting limitations to his propositions, where any are requisite; few in our own times, we might say in any times, could have accomplished what he has done.

Mr. Mill's principal works besides the " Analysis" already mentioned, are, 1, " The History of British India," not only the first work which has thrown the light of philosophy upon the people and upon the government of that

vast portion of the globe, but the first, and even
now the only work which conveys to the general
reader even that knowledge of facts, which,
with respect to so important a department of
his country's affairs, every Englishman should
wish to possess. The work is full of instructive
comments on the institutions of our own country, and abounds with illustrations of many of
the most important principles of government
and legislation.

2. " Elements of Political Economy." Mr.
Mill's powers of concatenation and systematic
arrangement peculiarly qualified him to place
in their proper logical connexion the elementary
principles of this science as established by its
great masters, and to furnish a compact and
clear exposition of them.

3. Essays on Government, Jurisprudence,
Education, &c. originally written for the Sup-
plement to the Encyclopædia Britannica ; the
most important of them have been several times
reprinted by private subscription.

These little works, most of which are mere
outlines to be filled up, though they have been
both praised and animadverted upon as if they
claimed the character of complete scientific
theories, have been, I believe, more read than
any other of Mr. Mill's writings, and have contributed more than any publications of our time
to generate a taste for systematic thinking on
the subject of politics, and to discredit vague
and sentimental declamation. The Essay on
Government, in particular, has been almost a
text-book to many of those who may be termed
the Philosophic Radicals. This is not the place
to criticise either the treatise itself or the criticisms of others upon it. Any critical estimate
of it thoroughly deserving the name, it has not

yet been my fortune to meet with; for Mr. Macauley—assuming, I suppose, the divine prerogative of genius—only entered the contest, in
order to carry away the argument he protected
in a cloud of words.

Mr. Mill's more popular writings are remarkable for a lofty earnestness, more stern
than genial, and which rather flagellates or
shames men out of wrong, than allures them to
the right.   Perhaps this is the style most natural to a man of deep moral convictions, writing
in an age and in a state of society like that in
which we live.   But it seems, also, to be con-
genial to the character of his own mind; for he
appears, on most occasions, much more strongly
alive to the evil of what is evil in our destiny,
than to the good of what is good.   He rather
warns us against the errors that tend to make us
miserable, than affords us the belief that by
any means we can attain to much positive happiness.   He does not hope enough from human
nature—something despondent and unelevating
clings round his estimate of its powers.   He
saddens the Present by a reference to the Past—
he does not console it by any alluring anticipations of the Future;—he rather discontents us
with vice than kindles our enthusiasm for virtue.   He possesses but little of

> " The vision and the faculty divine;"—

nor is it through his writings, admirable as
they are, that we are taught

> " To feel that we are greater than we know."

## THE END.

LONDON: PRINTED BY SAMUEL BENTLEY  DORSET-STREET.